Noah's Ark – Pitched and Parked

Noah's Ark – Pitched and Parked

Nathan M. Meyer

915.66
M575
Cop.2

BMH Books

Winona Lake, Indiana 46590

DEDICATED TO

THE MEMORY OF A DEAR FRIEND

ONE OF THE GREAT MEN OF OUR TIME

THE LATE

DR. RALPH E. CRAWFORD

Cover design and art: Alice Hoover

First printing: February 1977
Second printing: April 1977

ISBN: 0-88469-039-3

Printed in U.S.A.

Explanation of the Dedication

Dr. Ralph E. Crawford was a most remarkable man who, after he should have been retired, founded Search Foundation and threw himself completely into the project of searching for Noah's Ark. He was certain "the Ark is up there" and that God will reveal it just before the second coming of Christ. In pursuit of this goal he labored day and night, maintaining a grueling schedule that belied his 74 years.

He associated with princes and paupers alike; he was a nobleman at heart. He could have been wealthy but he gave it all away; he was generous to a fault. He walked among the mighty but he never lost the common touch. He loved the Lord and he loved His Word; he was a Christian gentleman in every sense of the word. He was my friend before he knew me and afterward as well.

He loved books as few men do and I am honored that the manuscript of this book should have been ordained of God to be the last one he would ever read. After we buried his body on November 5, 1976, amidst the autumnal splendor of the beautiful Maryland hills, Mrs. Crawford and I found my manuscript on his desk. I wondered if he had read it before the angels summoned his departure. How delighted I was to find his critique.

Over one chapter he wrote, "Excellent!" Another chapter was marked, "Super excellent!" Yet a third chapter carried this comment: "Fantastic—with one or two comments." But no one will ever know what those comments were. He left this world very suddenly to keep an appointment with the Lord whom he loved.

His last words to me were, "I want you to show the film in Wichita; I'll call you back within 48 hours." But in 48 hours he was in a casket.

Many times he had said during the six years I knew him, "Brother, the Lord brought us together."

And I would always answer, "That's true." And now I must add, "And the Lord took us apart." But I have the assurance that we shall soon meet again—after God has vindicated His Word to the world—by uncovering the Ark of Noah.

Acknowledgments

Grateful acknowledgement is hereby given to Alice Hoover, artist, draftsman, and student of the Bible to whom the author is greatly indebted for her interest and effort involving many hours of dedicated and tedious use of her God-given talents in preparing the longevity chart, sketches and drawings which appear in this book. And I am profoundly grateful for her artistry in designing and executing the unique cover of this book.

I am also greatly indebted to Bart LaRue for the benefit I have derived from the extensive and expensive research which he undertook in conjunction with the production of the film: *The Ark of Noah.*

Finally, I wish to express my deep gratitude to my loving wife, Mary, who typed and retyped this manuscript as often as necessary until it was finally finished.

The Purpose of This Book

This book is an attempt to provide answers to the questions people ask regarding the story of the Ark. Many questions come from teenagers. The answers, therefore, are simple enough so even they can understand them.

Since 1970, through circumstances not of my choosing, I have become involved in the search for Noah's Ark. For six years now, I have lectured on the subject on an average of nearly once a week. Usually the audience has been in a church, a school, or an auditorium, varying in size from a few dozen to a few hundred to a few thousand. But many times it has been a radio or television audience. Usually these have been interviews of the talk-show variety involving open-mike broadcasts where people are invited to call the station and ask questions.

I enjoy this activity because I find satisfaction in answering questions for which people want answers. I have found many of the answers and I enjoy sharing them with people who, in turn benefit from receiving them. So many have expressed deep appreciation for finally getting answers to questions which have frustrated them for many years.

Recently the producers of the film *The Ark of Noah* have allowed me to show the film in places of my choosing. So we are now using this professional documentary as an additional means of telling the world the story of the Flood and the search for Noah's Ark. But even this film leaves many questions unanswered, hence the necessity of this book.

The author has an extensive Bible conference ministry, and a special feature of each service is the opening of his camel bag containing items which
are used as object lessons for the children in the audience.

Table of Contents

PART I

THE STORY

OF THE

FLOOD

1

Are You Sure
There Was a Flood?

We have overwhelming evidence to indicate a catastrophic deluge in some remote period of earth's history. The evidence lies in *Tradition, Archaeology, History,* and of course, the *Bible.*

THE EVIDENCE OF TRADITION

Almost every tribe and nation on earth has a tradition in the form of a legend telling of a great flood that once destroyed most of the human race.

A few decades ago, Benjamin Allen, working in his humble Los Angeles trailer home, did a lot of research compiling 50 or 60 different legends involving that many different cultures—all of which told the story of a great flood and an ark.

More than 100 years ago the geologist, Hugh Miller, wrote his *Testimony of the Rocks* in which he expressed the conclusion that it is a universal tradition that in an early age of the world's history "well nigh the human race" was destroyed by a flood.

Years before that, the famous German naturalist, Alexander van Humboldt, traveled the world penetrating remote regions of the earth, contacting unknown tribes in primitive wildernesses. He found that invariably they all had a belief in a great deluge.

In most of these legends, details vary greatly but the basic story is there. Elements of these various traditions have so much in common that it is not reasonable to suppose they happened by chance. These elements include: A sinful human race, divine judgment involving universal destruction by water and one good family saved along with "seed" animals and birds to restore the animal kingdom. Usually survival is by a boat of some sort. A few times it is by a high mountain.

Here are the names of some of the nations, tribes, cultures, and religions listed as having such legends: Egyptians, Greeks, Romans, Hindus, Chinese, English, Druids, Greenlanders, Mexicans, Indians, Americans, Babylonians, Persians, Phrygians, Fiji Islanders, Polynesians, Brazilians, Peruvians, Welsh, Lithuanians, Finnish, Lapps, Serbians, Magyars, Burmeese, Filipinos, Massai, Eskimos, Aztecs, Chileans, Amazonians, Austrailians, Cubans, Tahitians, Scandinavians, Armenians, Kurds, Moslems, and of course Christians.

How could it be that all branches of the human race and all major religions, however remote, isolated, and out of contact they may be, have a similar story in their repertoire of traditions? Is it rational to shrug one's shoulders and simply say: "So what? Everybody has a legend and the Bible story is just one more among all the rest."

Or is it more reasonable to believe that the Bible has the real factual account of what happened and all the others are hand-me-down legends based on the original facts but told and retold so often with additions and deletions from century to century, partly by accident and partly by design. After all, is it not natural that people in each culture would try to reconcile and accommodate each detail to the theological beliefs of their own culture?

When one considers how a story today changes quickly when told and retold through several gossipers, it is amazing that all these legends have so much in common.

At any rate, if there were only a few such legends, we could dismiss the evidence. But when it is such a consistent and universal phenomenon among all races, nations, and religions, it would seem reasonable to a thinking, open-minded, unprejudiced person that all of these accounts stem from an actual historical event.

Imagine, if you can, the impact of such an event upon the lives of Noah's three sons. Next to creation it was the most impressive happening in the history of the world. Would they not have told their children and their grandchildren every detail over and over again?

And when the sons were separated and their posterity increased and developed into new races, nations, and religions, would not this story continue on for millenniums to come? Thus, in time, the people (all descended from Noah's three sons) of remote islands and lost jungles would all have a similar story to tell about their ancestoral origin. That makes sense to me. I think that is exactly what happened.

But legends are the least of our evidences. Let's look now at the evidence of archaeology.

THE EVIDENCE OF ARCHAEOLOGY

In 1872 George Smith made a fantastic discovery. He found a stone tablet in the British Museum which told the story of a universal flood that was very much like the Biblical account. The tablet had been excavated in Babylon. It is now the famous Gilgamesh Epic.

More than 50 years later, Leonard Wooley conducted an archaeological excavation of Ur, the city of Abraham, in the Euphrates Valley. He found a layer of water-born sediment approximately ten feet thick. In his report he said: "Taking into consideration all the facts there could be no doubt that the flood of which we had thus found the only possible evidence was the Flood of Sumerian history and legend, the Flood on which is based the story of 'Noah.' "

Members of the various Search Foundation expeditions to the top of Mt. Ararat report finding tons of marine fossils at the 13,800 foot level. These included fish, crabs, clams, and other marine animals. In 1964 the late Harry "Bud" Crawford, while leading one of those expeditions, found enormous quantities of rock sea-salt at the same level. It is obvious that this involved inundation of this high mountain for a period of many days to allow sufficient time for the salt to settle and crystalize into hard rock layers.

Rock salt crystals found at the 13,500 foot level on Mt. Ararat and verified to be sea salt. A sample of the enormous quantity found on the mountain.

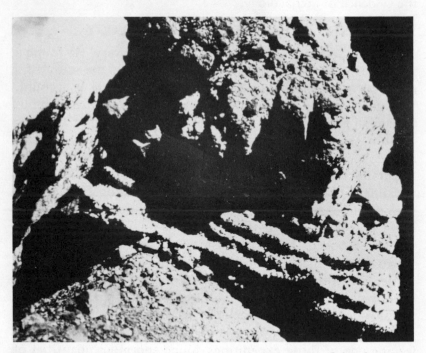

Marine fossils on Mt. Ararat. The strata in the lower part of the picture reveal tons of fossilized fish, snails, crabs and clams. *(Photo courtesy of Search Foundation.)*

It is my conviction that the whole study of fossils and geological layers cannot be adequately explained apart from a worldwide cataclysmic deluge not many thousands of years ago. All the fossils, including dinosaurs, are found in sedimentary rock, which rock, all agree, had its origin in the sediment laid down by water.

The facts involved in this whole matter are exciting and the evidence is overwhelming. For those who are interested, I suggest a most interesting little book, *The Great Dinosaur Mistake*, by my friend, Kelly Segraves. It is written in simple language so any teenager can understand it. (See page 112). The author presents many down-to-earth fascinating details in simple language, and I doubt you will be able to lay it down once you start reading it. It really makes the theory of evolution look foolish.

In the new exciting film, *The Ark of Noah*, produced by Bart LaRue and Jack Grimm, Mr. LaRue tells the story of a series of stones on the slope of Mt. Ararat arranged in a straight line leading up to the place where Mr. Navarra found a lot of pitch-soaked timber on what he calls the Navarra site. These stones have eight crosses on them and are said by archaelogists to be of Sumerian origin, perhaps 4,000 years old.

Mr. LaRue reports that pilgrimages were made up the mountain to the Ark as long ago as 4,000 years. Steps and special stones had been arranged for the convenience of pilgrims as well as a monastery in the foothills which served as a hostel. The ravages of time and earthquakes have removed or disarranged these things but rocks with crosses can still be seen today. The eight crosses are believed to represent the eight people kept alive in the Ark.

John Morris, in his book, *Adventure On Ararat*, tells of seeing these crosses etched in stone. He describes an ancient man-made cave carved out of rock near the town of Dougubeyazit, a Turkish town at the foot of Mt. Ararat. He also tells of a stone altar and inscriptions of various sorts carved in the rocks.

In her very excellent book, *Noah's Ark: Fact or Fable?*, Violet Cummings gives an interesting account of these inscriptions:

To Col. Koor—scholar, researcher, author, historian, and etymologist of ancient languages; a specialist in the ancient history of Russia and the Far East, as well as a graduate of the Czarist Military Academy of Kazan—belongs the important discovery in 1915 of the ancient Sumerian inscription at Karada near Greater Ararat, on the Araratsky Pass. This inscription tells about the Great Flood of the Bible, and was published by Dr. J. O. Kinnaman, director of the Bureau of Bible Research, in his magazine, *The Bible Archaeological Digest*, in the last quarter of 1946. Although several of the pictorial figures on the cliff had been defaced with the passing of the centuries, the story of the Deluge is clear:

"God sowed the seeds of the word into the waters . . . the waters filled the earth, descending from above . . . his children came to rest on the mountain or peak."

Regarding the authenticity of the translation of this remarkable inscription, Dr. Kinnaman wrote on August 2, 1946: "I have received two letters from Col. Koor . . . and have read and surveyed them critically . . . Col. Koor proves himself a scholar of high degree of attainment. Being familiar with Babylonian cuneiform, Egyptian heiroglyphics, Hebrew, etc., I would say that Col. Koor has made very accurate translations of the inscriptions he set out to interpret."

Mrs. Cummings also refers to the crosses and a huge stone face carved out of the mountain looking toward the site where the Ark is believed to be:

The two men made their way around the brow of the hill to the base of the structure on its lower side. Here they discovered a large rock adorned with eight beautifully carved crosses, guarding the entrance to what appeared to them a tumbled-in subterranean cave. Other inscriptions and crosses could also be distinguished on the other ruins at the site.

Silhouetted against the sky at the crest of a rocky eminence some distance away, the sharply carved outlines of a nobly proportioned patriarchal head rose perhaps 8 to 10 feet above the top of the hill. For some reason, the ancient sculptor had faced the bearded, turbaned profile so that its sightless gaze would forever rest on the towering heights of Aghri Dagh . . . ! (*Author's note:* Aghri Dagh is the Turkish name for Mt. Ararat.)

The latest evidence of archaeology is so recent most people haven't yet heard of it. There is a full-page account in *TIME* magazine (last week of October, 1976). A team of Italian archaeologists were digging in the ruins of Ebla (a city-state north of Damascus in Syria) when they uncovered one of the most exciting discoveries in the history of archaeology. More than 15,000 clay tablets in perfect state of preservation have been uncovered. They are dated very definitely about 2400 B.C. or several hundred years before Abraham. They give fantastic proof to the Biblical record of that ancient time. Those who have learned to take the Bible literally have cause for great rejoicing. Of course, most of these tablets have yet to be read but many Biblical names of people and places have already been found. *And there is at least one tablet telling the story of the Flood!*

THE EVIDENCE OF HISTORY

In chapter 15 I will answer the question: What makes you think the Ark is still up there? At that time I'll give the historical record involving over 200 people who claimed they saw the Ark. Of course, if the Ark is still there, that's the best proof we can get that the Flood actually took place.

THE EVIDENCE FROM THE BIBLE

The Book of Genesis tells the story in great detail. Chapter 5 introduces us to Noah's ancestors all the way back to Adam, giving each man's name, age, and other interesting details. Chapters 6 through 9 give the complete story of the Flood and its consequences. Chapters 10 and 11 present a list of Noah's descendants all the way to Abraham with many details about their activities, including their geographical habitation.

That's a total of seven chapters, out of the oldest history book in existence, devoted to the story of the Deluge and the people involved before, during, and after the Flood. There is absolutely no comparable literature in existence. No detail has ever been disproved. Many details have been verified from archaeological diggings.

The famous archaeologist, Dr. Nelson Glueck, says it this way: "It may be stated categorically that no archaeological discovery has ever controverted a Biblical reference. Scores of archaeological finds have been made which confirm in clear outline or in exact detail historial statements in the Bible."

Furthermore, it is interesting to note that there is no book in existence other than the Bible that tells us anything about the history of the world before the Flood. If such books were written they must have been destroyed in the Flood.

The Book of Genesis, written by Moses, tells how God told Noah, 120 years in advance, to build an Ark and prepare for the coming cataclysm. Noah did exactly what God told him and in due time all was ready.

When the appointed day arrived, Noah and his family and all the specified animals went into the Ark and God shut the door.

They had exactly one week to plan and practice all their chores involved in Ark-living. Then it started to rain. And, oh, how it did rain! Forty days and forty nights of the heaviest rainfall ever to pour out of the sky! And that's exactly what it did. The water *poured* out of the sky like out of a sluice or trough. But the Ark was not yet floating.

After the rain stopped, the waters out of the oceans (great deep) caused the depth of the flood-waters to increase severely so that the Ark began to float. The waters continued to rise for many days until the entire earth was flooded. In chapter 8 I will explain how I believe this happened.

One hundred fifty days passed from the time it started to rain until the waters receded sufficiently to allow the Ark to come to rest on a high mountain. However, Noah and his family were actually in the Ark a little over one year.

Noah, his family, and all the animals finally emerged into a new world. They had instructions to "breed abundantly in the earth . . . be fruitful and multiply. . . ."

The first thing Noah did was to build an altar and worship God who had so wonderfully saved him and his family.

At that point God put a rainbow in the sky for the first time in the history of planet Earth and told Noah it was a perpetual token of His promise never again to destroy the earth with a universal flood.

But Moses was not the only Biblical author to speak of the Flood. Samuel, Isaiah, Ezekiel, Job, Matthew, Luke, Peter, Paul, and Jesus all believed in Noah and spoke about him and/or the Flood.

The man, Noah, patriarch of the Flood, is referred to *by name* 54 times in the Bible—46 times in the Old Testament and 8 times in the New. Of course, that's not counting Noah's offspring named after him. Other verses speak of the Flood without mentioning Noah's name in the same verse but the reference is very clear just the same:

Job 22:15-16 refers to "wicked men ... cut down out of time ... overflown with a flood."

I Chronicles 1:4 gives the geneology of Noah.

Isaiah 54:9 quotes God saying: "... for I have sworn that the waters of Noah should no more go over the earth. ...."

Ezekiel 14:14, 20 mentions Noah, Daniel and Job, saying in effect that even these three great men could not help sinners escape the judgment of God in the days of the prophet Ezekiel.

Hebrews 11:7 Paul writes: "By faith Noah, being warned of God of things not seen as yet, moved with fear, prepared an ark to the saving of his house; by the which he condemned the world, and became heir of the righteousness which is by faith."

I Peter 3:20 "Which sometime were disobedient, when once the longsuffering of God waited in the days of Noah, while the ark was a preparing, wherein few, that is, eight souls were saved by water."

II Peter 2:5 "And spared not the old world, but saved Noah the eighth person, a preacher of righteousness, bringing in the flood upon the world of the ungodly."

II Peter 3:5-6 "For this they willingly are ignorant of, that by the word of God the heavens were of old, and the earth standing out of the water and in the water:
Whereby the world that then was, being overflowed with water, perished."

In the books bearing their names and authored by Matthew and Luke, Jesus is quoted making some very definite statements indicating that He believed in Noah, the Ark and the Flood:

Matthew 24:37-39 "But as the days of Noe were, so shall also the coming of the Son of man be.
For as in the days that were before the flood they were eating and drinking, marrying and giving in marriage, until the day that Noe entered into the ark,
And knew not until the flood came, and took

them all away; so shall also the coming of the Son of man be."

Luke 17:26-27   "And as it was in the days of Noe, so shall it be also in the days of the Son of man.

They did eat, they drank, they married wives, they were given in marriage, until the day that Noe entered into the ark, and the flood came, and destroyed them all."

Thus the Biblical record is clearly presented with no room for doubt, except on the part of those who doubt or deny the Bible itself. And anyone who does that, it seems to me, exposes his ignorance of the Bible. Who but a fool would dare to line himself up against such a formidable array of witnesses as we have presented, ranging all the way from Moses to Jesus?

The evidence seems overwhelming that there really was a great flood, just like the Bible says.

2

Why Did the
Flood Take Place?

SINFUL MORTALS

The answer is easy: because of sin. The human race had become so extremely wicked, a righteous, holy God could tolerate man's evil no longer. They had corrupted everything God had made.

Read carefully what Moses wrote in Genesis 6, verses 5, 11-13:

> And God saw that the *wickedness* of man was great in the earth, and that every imagination of the thoughts of his heart was only *evil* continually.
>
> The earth also was *corrupt* before God, and the earth was filled with *violence*.
>
> And God looked upon the earth, and, behold, it was *corrupt*; for all flesh had *corrupted* his way upon the earth.
>
> And God said unto Noah, the end of all flesh is come before me; for the earth is filled with *violence* through them; and, behold, I will destroy them with the earth.

Notice the key words: wickedness, evil, corruption, and violence. These words are used to describe the sinfulness of the human race in the days before the Flood. God looks and then

God speaks. Verse 12 says:

> And *God looked* upon the earth, and, behold, it was corrupt; for all flesh had corrupted his way upon the earth.

Verse 13 continues: "And *God said* . . . I will destroy them."

In God's announcement we can clearly see that the cause of the Flood was awful sin on the part of the people whom God had made and the final outcome was death by drowning.

SINFUL ANGELS

Not only were human beings involved but I believe fallen angels were also in the picture. Both Peter and Jude talk about evil angels in connection with the Flood.

In II Peter 2:4 Peter tells us of the severe judgment of God upon "the angels that sinned." He says these angels were cast "down . . . to hell [hades] and delivered them into chains of darkness, to be reserved unto judgment; and spared not the old world, but saved Noah . . . bringing in the flood. . . ."

Who are these angels that are held in chains of darkness in hades and how were they connected with the Flood?

Look what Jude, the brother of Jesus, writes in Jude 6 and 7:

> And the angels which kept not their first estate, but left their own habitation, he hath reserved in everlasting chains under darkness unto the judgment of the great day.
>
> Even as Sodom and Gomorrha, and the cities about them in like manner, giving themselves over to fornication, and going after strange flesh, are set forth for an example, suffering the vengeance of eternal fire.

Jude is undoubtedly speaking of the same angels.

Notice the facts presented in these accounts:

1. These angels sinned—they are not the holy angels.
2. They are a *special* group of evil angels since they are confined—not free to roam like the main body of fallen angels.
3. Their sin involved leaving their "first estate"—the estate of angels. They left their own habitation—they departed from living in the realm assigned to them.
4. They did like Sodom and Gomorrha "in like manner, giving themselves over to fornication, and going after *strange flesh*. . . ."
5. Their sin was so terrible they were confined immediately

in chains, in darkness, in hades—to remain there until the final judgment when they will be cast into the lake of fire.

Now who could they be? They are a special group of angels not otherwise mentioned in the Bible.

Originally God created myriads of angels in heaven—each created individually without sin. Then He gave them the choice to love or reject their creator. A vast number, including Lucifer, rebelled and were cast out of heaven. Under Lucifer's leadership all the fallen angels as disembodied spiritual beings called demons, took up their abode in the air and space where Satan is called the "prince of the power of the air."

Angels are always referred to in the masculine gender, but Jesus makes it clear they never marry. So what were Peter and Jude talking about? I think we have the answer in the story of the "sons of God" in the flood account of Genesis 6:1-4:

> And it came to pass, when men began to multiply on the face of the earth, and daughters were born unto them,
> That the sons of God saw the daughters of men that they were fair; and they took them wives of all which they chose (vv. 1-2).

The phrase "sons of God" is used six times in the New Testament. Without a doubt, in every case the reference is to human beings who have been saved by faith in Christ.

This same exact phrase is used five times in the Old Testament, twice in the flood story of Genesis 6, and three times in the Book of Job. (The phrase "sons of the living God" appears once in Hosea 1:10 in which a prophecy is made announcing what saved Jews in the future kingdom would be called, namely: Sons of the Living God.) The three passages in Job are crystal clear in that they refer to angels including the fallen angel, formerly Lucifer, but after the fall called Satan.

Job 1:6:

> Now there was a day when the sons of God came to present themselves before the LORD, and Satan came also among them.

Job 2:1 (Same verse with the first word changed to "again"):

> Again there was a day when the sons of God came to present themselves before the LORD, and Satan came also among them to present himself before the LORD.

The third passage in Job is chapter 38, verse 7. God is asking the question in verse 4: "Where wast thou when I laid the foundations of the earth?" And in verse 7 He continues: "When the morning stars sang together, and *all* the sons of God shouted for joy?"

This last reference clearly refers to all the angels at the time of creation and before the Fall. Job 1:6 and 2:1 seem to refer to both holy angels and sinful angels, Satan being one of the latter group.

Now let's look at the remaining two references in Genesis 6.

Verse 2 says, ". . . the sons of God saw the daughters of men . . . ." And verse 4 says, ". . . the sons of God came in unto the daughters of men, and they bare children. . . ."

So who are the sons of God here? Are they angels also? If angels are sexless and never marry as Jesus said, then how could these sons of God be angels?

Here is the explanation that I think satisfies and harmonizes all the Scriptures without contradiction. At least it satisfies me; I hope it does the same for my readers.

Yes, the angels as angels are sexless and they never marry. They were not made to procreate as are members of the human race. For our information I must add that angels are always referred to in the masculine gender, never female.

It appears to me that when we put together all the facts of Jude, Peter, and Genesis 6 that we have a most unusual situation, a once-in-all-time occurrence.

I think some (not all) fallen angels used the supernatural power which God allowed them and materialized themselves as men, appearing with human bodies.

We have the clear record of this happening in Genesis 19. God sent "two angels" (since they were obeying God, they were certainly holy angels) to destroy Sodom. But when they entered the city, Lot recognized them *as men.* They washed the dust from their feet, entered Lot's house as male guests, feasted on Lot's food, and prepared to get a good night's rest. Two angels did all this. But there is more.

The unspeakable wickedness of Lot's neighbors is evident by the way they demanded the privileges of having homosexual relations with "these men." Lot refused their request, offering his daughters to them instead. This offer was rejected and they prepared to batter down Lot's front door. At that point the two angels, appearing as men, ended the whole shameful episode by using their supernatural power to strike all the evil attackers with blindness.

The next morning when the "two men" had led Mr. and Mrs. Lot and their two daughters out of town, fire and brimstone fell and the whole wicked place was burned to a crisp. Be sure to read Genesis 19 and see for yourself.

The point I'm making is this: Angels in Old Testament times did have the ability to appear as mortal men. God commanded them to do so on various occasions in order to accomplish His purpose. I don't think they occupied existing bodies as demons ordinarily attempt to do, but I think they actually materialized into male bodies.

In the Flood account I believe we have fallen angels using such power totally contrary to God's will. I think they deliberately chose to leave their first estate, that of angels, and they materialized as men. They looked at the beautiful daughters of the human race, lusted after them, married them, and cohabited with them. Comparing what the angels did with what the wicked Sodomites did, Jude says "in like manner," "going after strange flesh." Now doesn't all that make sense?

But what was the outcome? It was this intolerable tainting of the human race that provoked God into action. As we read in Genesis 6:3, God announced that His patience had reached the breaking point. The decision for judgment and destruction had been forced upon Him. The end is announced, allowing only sufficient time for Noah to cut the trees and build the Ark.

Genesis 6:3:

> And the Lord said, My spirit shall not always strive with man, for that he also is flesh: yet his days shall be an hundred and twenty years.

But there is more to the story. The offspring of this unholy union were monsters. The Hebrew word for giants in verse 4 is *nephthalim* or fallen ones, and that they surely were. But the rest of the verse tells us they were so big and strong; they were famous everywhere. So it comes out the same way no matter how you translate *nephthalim*. The offspring were giants.

Genesis 6:4:

> There were giants in the earth in those days; and also after that, when the sons of God came in unto the daughters of men, and they bare children to them, the same became mighty men which were of old, men of renown.

Why did the Flood take place? The Biblical answer is: Because of the extreme wickedness of mortals and angels. If God wanted to preserve the human race, He had no other choice but to bring judgment and destroy all except the one righteous family remaining alive on earth. He could have chosen any one of a number of methods to accomplish His purpose but in His omniscience, He chose the Deluge.

3

Did the World
Have Any Warning?

Again the answer is clear and definite. The world had plenty of warning. Unfortunately they deliberately chose to ignore the warning.

God is a loving God, not willing that any should perish. So in Genesis 6:13-14 He quickly proceeds to follow His announcement of *punishment for sinners* with an announcement of His *provision for salvation* freely offered to all who accept.

Peter calls Noah "a preacher of righteousness" (II Peter 2:5). Even though he had no converts outside of his own family, faithful Noah went on preaching for 120 years (Gen. 6:3) and Noah believed what he preached. He was no hypocrite. As we say, he put his money where his mouth was. For all the while he was preaching, he was also working on the Ark. Read again what the writer to the Hebrews says in chapter 11, verse 7.

> By faith Noah, being warned of God of things not seen as yet, moved with fear, prepared an ark to the saving of his house; by the which he condemned the world, and became heir of the righteousness which is by faith.

Notice that Noah took God seriously. He believed God when

God warned him about the Flood. Long before the water started to fall, Noah labored to make preparation as per God's detailed instructions. The rest of the wicked world undoubtedly mocked and ridiculed Noah and his message but in the final outcome they had condemned themselves to the doom of the Deluge.

In Genesis 4 we are given a picture of the sinful background by the mention of specific sins that were corrupting earth's mortals. Cain committed murder and thereafter stayed as far away from God as he possibly could. He "went out from the presence of the Lord . . ." (v. 16). From then on it was the practice of his descendants to ignore God and deliberately live in willful sin, even being so brazen as to boast about it. We see polygamy in verse 19 and murder in verse 23 as well as verse 8. They were living for pleasure, having chosen to rebel against God as they defied His authority and His will by their sensual, sinful, wicked ways.

God told them that He would not tolerate their rebellion indefinitely. Genesis 6:3 says: "And the LORD said, My spirit shall not always strive with man, for that he also is flesh: yet his days shall be an hundred and twenty years."

God gave them 120 years to repent and told them not only the punishment but also the length of probation, so they wouldn't be caught unawares and therefore unprepared. But nobody listened and nobody cared.

They rejected Noah, his message, and his God. By the time they knew that Noah was right; it was too late. What sad words: *Too late!*

Observe what Jesus had to say about this whole, sad situation.

AS WERE THE DAYS OF NOAH

But as the days of Noe were, so shall also the coming of the Son of man be.

For as in the days that were before the flood they were eating and drinking, marrying and giving in marriage, until the day that Noe entered into the ark,

And knew not until the flood came, and took them all away; so shall also the coming of the Son of man be (Matt. 24:37-39).

"As the days of Noe [Noah] were"! How were they? The

people were eating and drinking and getting married. What's wrong with that? Nothing, except that as they followed their daily materialistic routine of living, they were totally oblivious to their impending doom. Even on the morning of the last day, they *didn't know* that the cataclysmic deluge was only hours away. The world was to be covered with water, and all of them would be drowned in the angry waters of the greatest flood of all time. And they didn't know it. They were planning weddings, honeymoons, banquets, and so on. And they didn't know!

Why didn't they know? It wasn't because the warning had not been sounded. Everybody had heard the prediction from the "crazy preacher," Noah. But nobody believed him. Everybody thought that Noah was an eccentric old man with a lot of foolish ideas.

He said water was actually going to fall out of the sky. How ridiculous! Nobody had ever heard of anything so outlandish. After all, it had never happened in the past and even in that ancient time they taught their children that "the past is the key to the future." From creation until now it had never rained.

> . . . for the LORD God had not caused it to rain upon the earth . . . .
> But there went up a mist from the earth, and watered the whole face of the ground.
> And a river went out of Eden to water the garden . . . (Gen. 2:5, 6, 10).

It is obvious that it had never rained up to now and the people therefore assumed that it never would. And, of course, it follows that there were no clouds in the sky; no thunderstorms ever disturbed man's paradise, and there were no tornadoes, no hurricanes, no winds.

To make Noah's message sound even more foolish, we must remember that Noah said that the coming flood would cover the whole earth. It was to be a universal deluge. There was no way to escape even by climbing the highest mountain. The only place of refuge was to be the safety of the Ark.

But the Ark itself must have been the brunt of vicious ridicule. Imagine building a barge out of hand-hewed logs so colossal in size it would be the biggest all-wood barge of all time.

And then, to top it all, Noah was making no provision for launching his monstrous creation. There it rested on the Mesopotamian plain. The boat—half as big as the *Queen Mary*, one and one-half times as long as a football field; with no way to get it into the water.

Of course Noah had no problem on that score. He really believed what God said. God said He would send a flood and Noah knew the Ark would float. But when Noah told the people what God said, their laughter must have been hilarious.

In rejecting Noah's unusual message, they must have made great sport of Noah's preaching. I think they were laughing all up and down the Euphrates Valley at that crazy preacher who really believed water would fall out of the sky. I can imagine Noah-jokes were the popular source of merriment.

They must have been cruel, scoffing, abusive, Madalyn O'Hair-type, Satan-inspired. Not in any way like some of the harmless, good-natured humor we hear from time to time like this one:

Two little boys were talking about the story of the Flood. Their conversation went something like this.

First Boy: Just think of the good time Noah had all during the Flood.

Second Boy: What do you mean?

First Boy: Well, with nothing to do and no place to go, he could go fishing every day, all day long.

Second Boy: Oh, I don't think so. Remember he had only two worms.

To people living in a paradise of pleasant sun-glow and tropical gardens with a few beautiful crystal-clear rivers, the idea of a deluge must have seemed completely impossible. Therefore anybody who would predict such a stupid thing must certainly be out of his mind. Consequently nobody (not a single person outside of his own family) believed him.

But Noah did not stand alone; think for a moment of his father and grandfather. His father, Lamech, died only five years before the Flood, at the age of 777. His grandfather, Methuselah, died the same year as the Flood, at the age of 969. His very name means "when he is dead, it shall be sent." He was the oldest man who ever lived. It is interesting to note that

Methuselah was born 238 years *before Adam died.* Just think of all the long talks these two men must have had over that long period.

And then consider what a good time Grandpa Methuselah had telling his favorite grandson, Noah, everything he had learned from Adam who had walked and talked with God. Methuselah was 369 years old when Noah was born; so he and Noah were living at the same time over a span of 600 years. Noah must have heard his grandfather tell him about Adam and God and creation and sin so often that he knew all the details by heart. The year 1656 A.C. (after creation) was a mighty eventful year for Noah. It was the year his grandfather died and the year the Ark floated. Within months of his grandfather's funeral everybody on earth also died except Noah and his wife, their three sons and their wives—"eight righteous souls"—safe in the Ark. All his brothers and sisters and indeed all living relatives drowned in the flood in the same year. It was the world's worst catastrophe.

Noah had a lot to preach about and he could always get an "Amen" from his grandfather who was there—the only man alive during Noah's 120 years of warning, who had talked to Adam. Noah had never seen his great-grandfather, Enoch. But you can be sure he must have been excited many times as his father and grandfather told him all about how Enoch went to heaven without dying. That beats the story of rockets and "moonmen" any time.

In the Book of Jude we are told (vv. 14 and 15) that Enoch was a preacher, the seventh from Adam. The next preacher to be mentioned in the Bible in this line of preachers was Noah—two generations later. Peter calls him "a preacher of righteousness," the eighth one (II Peter 2:5). Maybe he means Noah was the eighth person to go into the Ark or maybe he is saying Noah was the eighth preacher since Adam. It's hard to say. But some things are very clear.

Jude, the brother of Jesus, tells us that Enoch preached about the coming of the Lord and the judgment of the ungodly (read Jude 14 and 15). Also, look at the chronology chart included with this book and observe that Adam must have been in the audience when Enoch preached about the coming of the

Lord. Imagine that! Enoch preached to Adam as well as to his own son Methuselah in the same audience.

Methuselah was a preacher's kid. He heard his father, Enoch, preach for 300 years. That's long enough to remember well enough to tell grandson Noah all about what he said. Then, too, we should mention that when Noah was born in the year 1056, even though grandfather Enoch had already gone to heaven, four of his older ancestors, in the godly line, were still alive. Noah talked with great, great grandfather Jared and with great, great, great grandfather Mahalaleel and with great, great, great, great grandfather Cainan and even with great, great, great, great, great grandfather Enos (Adam's grandson).

Think what a family reunion that must have been! Even with one grandpa in heaven, Noah had five living, godly grandpas to talk to, in addition to his father, not to mention all the grandmothers.

But it must have been a burden to these godly men to realize that thousands of relatives like brothers, sisters, nephews, nieces, uncles, aunts, cousins, and so forth and so on, were unsaved and would not listen to the preachers in the family. How sad!

Noah certainly had a good theological training with all those great preachers in the family who could speak with such overwhelming authority. And then to think that this training lasted 480 years (120 years before the Flood at which time Noah was 600 years old.)

Pity us poor preachers today who study in a seminary for a mere three or four years, reading a lot of books that are often written by confused commentators and writers copying what other men have said. But we do have something Noah didn't have. We have the complete written revelation from God called the Bible and that's why I can write and tell you all these things. It's all in the Bible. Even the "dry" chapters that deal with dates and numbers and chronology become fascinatingly interesting.

But Noah's preparation for preaching included another extremely important item. In Genesis 6:9 we read, ". . . Noah was a just man and perfect [blameless—not sinless] . . . and NOAH

WALKED WITH GOD." Therein lay Noah's secret. They could laugh and mock all they wanted. Noah knew he was right. He had walked with God. So he never once considered quitting. He went right on with his work—preaching and building. His whole life at this point was centered on one compelling dual task—to warn the world and prepare to escape the judgment. We can be sure the coming flood occupied his mind day and night.

And then one day it happened. Noah was ready, but the world was not. They were taking care of all the routine activities of their daily lives and knew not until the Flood came and took them all away.

Did they have any warning? Yes, indeed they did! Did they heed the warning? No indeed, they did not! They deliberately chose to be willfully ignorant. How sad! When it started to rain, it was too late.

4

How Could Noah Get All Those Animals in One Boat?

People say, "When I think of all the animals in the world, I don't believe a man could get so many in one boat even if he took only two of each kind." These people make two mistakes.

A. THEY THINK NOAH TOOK MORE ANIMALS THAN HE REALLY DID

In their minds they are compiling a list that could start out like this:

two Great Danes	two Dachshunds	two Collies
two German Shepherds	two Poodles	two Boxers
two Irish Setters	two Terriers	two Saint Bernards
two Bulldogs	two Scotties	two Beagles

At that rate they might fill the Ark with dogs. But Noah did not take two of every breed. He took two of each kind. Of all the dogs in the world, Noah took only two dogs. Of all the breeds and varieties of cats, Noah took only two cats. Of all the horses, he took only two horses. The same is true of cows, camels, and cougars. Of course, for food and sacrifice purposes after the Flood, Noah took seven of some kinds as God commanded him (Gen. 7:2).

At this point a question that invariably comes up is this: If Noah took only two dogs into the Ark, how is it we have so many different dogs today? The answer is simple.

God loves variety; He hates monotony. He never yet made two snowflakes alike. So He created into the reproductive apparatus of genes and chromosomes the possibility of endless hereditary combinations producing the possibility of endless variety within each "kind."

As long as man controls what he calls selective breeding he can produce German Shepherds, Black Angus cattle, and Appaloosa horses and keep the strain "pure" as he calls it. But if he allows each kind to live free in the natural habitat, these various breeds will disappear. They will never crossbreed between different kinds. Even so, there will be great variety among the whole family of any given kind.

Bear in mind that a "kind" is that specific group which will freely reproduce together—like all dogs, all cats, all lions, all tigers, all giraffes. But they never freely cross the mating line to produce a half-horse and half-cow or a half-elephant and half-buffalo, or a half-man and half-fish. There are no mermaids except in mythology.

God made each to produce after its kind and Noah took two of each kind into the Ark. All others were drowned. So all the animals on earth today—and some like the mammoth and dinosaur that have since become extinct—all came from the two of their kind that Noah took into the Ark.

By the same token all human beings on earth today are related—having come from the three sons of Noah and their wives.

The descendants of Cain all perished in the flood. Nobody on earth is related to him except as we trace our lineage back through Noah to Seth, son of Adam and brother of Cain. That settles once and for all the question: Did all the black people descend from Cain? The answer is: No, how could they? All of Cain's descendants drowned in the Flood.

But where did the races come from? Like I said, God loves variety and over the millenniums of time since Noah's day, all the races evolved from Shem, Ham, and Japheth, Noah's three sons. So we have people who are black, red, white, yellow, and many shades in between. That's a study all in itself, and we shall not pursue it further now.

B. PEOPLE DON'T REALIZE HOW BIG THE ARK WAS

The second mistake people make in connection with the problem of the capacity of the Ark is that they have no conception of how big the Ark really was.

GOD'S BLUEPRINT FOR THE ARK

Genesis 6:14-15:

> Make thee an ark of gopher wood; rooms shalt thou make in the ark, and shalt pitch it within and without with pitch.
> And this is the fashion which thou shalt make it of: The length of the ark shall be three hundred cubits, the breadth of it fifty cubits, and the height of it thirty cubits.

Noah didn't go to college to study the art of shipbuilding. He didn't make a model and run tests to find out which dimensions would work best for his project. He didn't waste any time on calculations of the proper proportion of the main dimensions. God told him exactly what to do. Any shipbuilder today will tell you (as one did to me in Baltimore) that the proportions Noah used were right. Shipbuilders still use them today.

God told Noah to make the Ark 300 cubits long, 50 cubits wide, and 30 cubits high.

Nobody knows the exact length of a cubit. In the days before standardized measuring sticks like rulers and yardsticks, the one thing every man always had available was his arm. So that was a cubit—the length of the forearm from the elbow to the tip of the fingers. Consequently writers have presented figures from 17 inches to 22 inches. Some even mentioned giants with forearms 3 feet long. I'm 6 feet 2 inches in height and my forearm is 20½ inches long.

The most commonly accepted length of a cubit, however, is 18 inches or 1½ feet. And this was the official length accepted by the Jews way back in the time when King Hezekiah dug his famous tunnel in Jerusalem nearly 700 years before Christ. The archaeologists found the inscription, put there by Hezekiah's

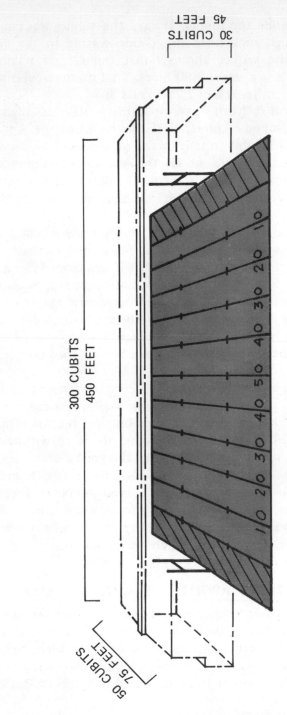

30 CUBITS
45 FEET

300 CUBITS
450 FEET

50 CUBITS
75 FEET

THE SIZE OF THE ARK COMPARED TO A FOOTBALL FIELD.

workmen, inside the tunnel. It says the tunnel was cut 1,200 cubits through rock from the Gihon Spring to the Pool of Siloam. I have walked through that tunnel and I know the length of it is just under 1,800 feet. That means a cubit was 1½ feet officially in Jerusalem 2,700 years ago.

What was it in Noah's day, probably a little less than 5,000 years ago? Nobody knows, yet! Maybe when the Ark is uncovered we'll be able to tell. In the meantime, let's use the 18 inches or 1½ foot figure and say the Ark was a minimum of 450 feet long. Some eyewitness accounts talk about the Ark being 500 feet in length, and if Noah was a big man that could easily be.

Even so, at a length of 450 feet, the Ark was monstrous—one and a half times as long as a football field. Imagine that!

All accounts seem to indicate that it was shaped like a barge. It was built to hold a huge cargo, not for speed. Noah wasn't going anywhere. Therefore, it had no sharp keel to ply the waters. What it had was capacity—room! Assuming it was 450 feet long, 75 feet wide and 45 feet high, the capacity of the Ark would have been equal to more than 500 railroad boxcars. And that's a lot of capacity.

The Ark had three floors with ceilings averaging 15 feet in height. With all the partitions, pens, walkways, cages, storage bins, and so forth, serving as internal bracing, the Ark must have been very strong as indeed it needed to be to withstand the storms, tidal waves, and upheavals of the great flood.

Remember, Noah needed no space for engine rooms, fuel tanks, and so forth, as do modern ocean liners. This means all the space was available for animals, food, water, and, of course, living quarters for Noah and his family. All calculations point to the fact that it was big enough to handle the job—the very special job of preserving life on planet Earth.

EVERYTHING ABOUT THE ARK WAS SPECIAL

A Special Designer gave Noah a special blueprint to build a special boat out of a special wood for a special voyage carrying a special cargo with a special crew—all for a special purpose. And a thousand years later, more or less, God inspired Moses to write a special account to be recorded in a special Book. And

Wood found by Search Foundation expedition on Mt. Ararat. The Bible calls it *gopher*, the natives call it *cypress*, the scientists call it *oak*. It is saturated with pitch (white streaks).

A $3,000 model built to scale from the Biblical description of the Ark and used by the producer, Bart LaRue, in the making of the film *The Ark of Noah*.

we must thank God that we have the special privilege of reading and possessing that Book—a privilege most people on earth do not have.

WHAT KIND OF WOOD
WAS USED TO MAKE THE ARK?

God calls it *gopher* wood. The scientists call it oak. The local people who live near Mt. Ararat call it cypress.

So take your choice: gopher, oak, cypress. The fact remains that such trees as were used to build the Ark do not grow any more. How do I know that? First of all let me say the wood found on Mt. Ararat believed to be a part of Noah's Ark is *hard* wood—very hard. There are no hardwood trees growing today within hundreds of miles of Mt. Ararat.

Evidently they used longer logs than could be made from hardwood trees today, regardless of where they might be found. In 1955 Mr. Navarra, the French industrialist and expert alpinist, found a huge hulk of black wood deep in an icy crevasse—50 tons of it that he could see. In the wall of the ice he said he could see one individual hand-hewed log that was about 150 feet long. He chopped into the ice and cut off a piece of it which he brought home with him.

Where on earth today could one find a hardwood tree tall enough to make a log 150 feet long? Maybe there are such trees somewhere in some remote jungle but certainly they are not commonly known. The redwoods of California, of course, grow to be 300 feet tall but they are soft wood, not hardwood. And they are a long way from the Euphrates Valley. By the way, the oldest redwood tree living today started growing about a thousand years after the Flood. Just for the record, in the Nevada Hotel in Ely, Nevada, there is on display a cross section of the oldest tree in existence, a bristlecone pine. (*Timberline Ancients* by Muench and Lambert. Charles Belding, Publisher). It has about 5,000 rings and, therefore, I think it started growing more than 500 years before the Flood.

The rings show a marked change at just about the time we believe the Flood occurred. Approximately 4,500 years ago, the rings suddenly changed in color and size. The change is from thick to very thin growth rings indicating a drastic change in climate at that point.

I think the drastic change of climate which I shall explain in the next chapter caused the Biblical gopher trees, those hardwood giants of the forest which Noah used to build the Ark, to become extinct.

Something else to remember about the wood: it was to be treated with pitch inside and out. God said, ". . . pitch it within and without with pitch." I would say, "Tar it within and without with tar."

WHERE DID NOAH GET THE TAR OR BITUMEN?

When Adam and Eve were driven out of the Garden of Eden in the land of the Tigris and Euphrates rivers, they migrated eastward as did their descendants after them. Noah lived in the Mesopotamian Valley or the valley of the Euphrates. Later it was called Babylon but before that Abraham had lived in the area.

In 1854 Abraham's ancient home town, Ur of the Chaldees, was excavated. Again in 1918 and also later, the archaeologists were busy. They learned a great many fascinating details. One very interesting fact was the name the Arabs used for this place: *Al Muqayyar* which means the "mound of bitumen." Today it is called Iraq and everybody knows that that part of the world is famous for its oil and bituminous products. So it would appear that Noah had no problem on that score. It was a natural resource in his area.

Of course, there is also the possibility that the pitch came from the resin of certain trees as some believe. Maybe so. At this point, who can say?

5

Why Did God Tell Noah
To Pitch the Ark?

That's a good question and an extremely important one. For the first 25 years of my serious Bible study I could not imagine why God would have told Noah to do something that seemed to me to be so utterly foolish and ridiculous.

I could understand why he should smear tar on the outside. To waterproof it of course. But why on the inside where it could serve no useful purpose but would rather be a constant source of irritation to the occupants of the Ark. Imagine having the entire inside of your house given a treatment of undercoating like your car. Let's hope the furniture was omitted. Maybe it was confined only to the main walls of the Ark.

At any rate, it never made sense to me as long as I knew nothing about the possibility of its preservation for thousands of years to come. When I learned about that the picture changed drastically. At first I was utterly skeptical. I could think of at least five good reasons why the idea of the Ark being in existence today had to be beyond the realm of possibility.

First of all, the wood couldn't possibly last so long. It would have rotted, deteriorated, and disintegrated many centuries ago.

In the second place, people would have cut it up for sacred souvenirs long ago. Nothing could possibly be left of it now. In the third place, the Bible does not mention one word about its preservation. In the fourth place, God would never have allowed it to be preserved until now lest religionists should make a shrine and an idol out of it. And one final bit of reasoning clinched the argument: We are saved by faith, not by sight; therefore, God would not allow such visible, absolute proof of the early chapters of Genesis. So I was sure there was no Ark of Noah in existence today.

But that was before I heard the evidence. Now I'm persuaded that I was wrong on all counts. I believe God deliberately planned to preserve it by having Noah cover it inside and out with a thick layer of bituminous pitch.

I was delighted to be able to satisfy my mind that God knew what He was doing. Of course, in my heart I knew all the time that God knew what He was doing. But I didn't know what He had planned, and so it didn't make sense to me. But now it does—very much so.

God told Noah to *pitch the Ark* so it would be preserved for nearly 5,000 years and then, as we shall see later, God *parked the Ark* in a special cove on a high, remote, cold, inaccessible mountain, waiting for that special day in history when it would best serve His purpose to reveal it to the world. I believe that day is about to dawn.

6

Was Noah Really
Six Hundred Years Old?

Noah was 600 years old at the time of the Flood. That's what the Bible says. "And Noah was six hundred years old when the flood of waters was upon the earth" (Gen. 7:6). The Bible is very plain. There is no question about what it says. Noah was 600 years old.

BUT WERE THEIR YEARS
THE SAME AS OURS TODAY?

First of all, let's look at their use of the shorter units of time—days, weeks, and months and ask a similar question.

The first chapter of Genesis says that God made the world in six days and rested on the seventh day. How long was a day? There are many arguments but I don't think there should be. I think the Bible is very clear. Verse 5 ends with this sentence: "And the evening and the morning were the first day." Verses 8, 13, 19, 23, 31 all conclude with the exact same words describing days 2, 3, 4, 5, 6. Then chapter 2 begins:

Thus the heavens and the earth were finished, and all the host of them.

And on the seventh day God ended his work which he had made; and he rested on the seventh day from all his work which he had made.

And God blessed the seventh day, and sanctified it: because that in it he had rested from all his work which God created and made.

What could be clearer? One evening and one morning were included in each day—no more, no less. A day of creation as recorded in the Book of Genesis had to be the time allowed to see one sunrise and one sunset—essentially a 24-hour day. Anybody who stretches it to 1,000 years or any other length of time is doing so on the basis of his arbitrary reasoning—not on the basis of what the Bible says. Their day was the same as ours.

WAS THEIR WEEK THE SAME AS OURS?

Seven of these days are combined in a unit of time used all the way through the Bible. The Hebrew word for week is the word "seven," sometimes used to refer to a week of days, sometimes to a week of years. For example, Jacob worked seven years for Leah and then had to work another time that long to fulfill Rachael's "week" also—fourteen years in all.

But we commonly use the word "week" today to refer to seven days. Ever since creation there have been seven days in a week. So I'm sure a week in Noah's time was the same as ours is today.

WHAT ABOUT THEIR MONTH?

Genesis 7:11 says the Flood started on the 17th day of the second month. On our calendar that would be February 17. But, of course, they had different names for months. In Genesis 8:4 we are told that the Ark came to rest "in the seventh month, on the seventeenth day of the month." That would have been exactly 5 months to the day. Now compare Genesis 7:24, and we are told this same period was 150 days. If 5 months equaled 150 days, then they must have calculated 30 days to a month—just as we do today.

NOW, WHAT ABOUT THEIR YEARS?

I believe their years were the same, too. In the first place, observe some facts in Genesis 5. There were 10 patriarchs from Adam to Noah. Each man's name and his total age is given.

Methuselah, Noah's grandfather, is the oldest at 969. Noah's father, Lamech, is the youngest at 777. Noah, himself, is said to have lived 950 years. Of course, Enoch, Methuselah's father, went to heaven without dying in the prime of youth at the age of 365. Eliminating Enoch and counting only the ones who died, we calculate the average age of these men to be 912. This involved Noah and his ancestors before the Flood.

Now look in the same Book of Genesis at the list of Noah's descendants after the Flood. In chapter 11 we start with Noah's son, Shem, who died at the age of 600. His son was 438 and for 2 more generations each man named is just over 400. That's quite a drop from Noah at 950 to Shem at 600 and then down almost to 400. In just two generations the age of man was cut in half.

But that's not the end. In the very next generation it was cut in half again so that the age dropped to just over 200. This figure prevailed for the next 3 generations. Then we have another drastic drop to 148 (Nahor). The 5 generations that follow Nahor with their ages are these: Terah—205, Abram—175 (25:7), Isaac—180 (35:28), Jacob—147 (49:33), and Joseph—110 (50:22). Notice that in this list of 23 patriarchs from Adam to Joseph, their ages ranged all the way from 969 down to 110, an age sometimes attained in our present-day world.

Observe that all these figures are given in the same book written by the same author. Nobody questions the "years" of Joseph; they only question the "years" of the men who lived before the Flood, the ones who averaged 912.

Since this is all one account, would it be reasonable for the author of Genesis to change the meaning of the word "years" in the middle of his story? It certainly would not seem so. I think it must follow that the "years" in Genesis are all the same.

There is no evidence at all to indicate that in general they had a different year from what we have today.

COULD THE "YEARS" HAVE BEEN "MONTHS"?

The Genesis 5 account of the men of great longevity also includes the ages of these men when they became fathers. Here are their ages listed in order as given: 130, 105, 90, 70, 65, 162, 187, 182, 502. The first is Adam, the last is Noah. Some people have suggested that maybe these were months instead of years. But that can't be taken seriously, especially when we go to the other list in Genesis 11 and look at those figures: 100, 34, 30, 34, 30, 32, 30, 29, 70, 100. The first is Shem; the last is Abraham. Noah was 502 years old when Shem was born. That's the oldest of all at the birth of a son. If these figures were months instead of years, Noah would have been 41 years old. But what about Nahor who was only 29 when Terah was born. If it were 29 months, Nahor actually would have been less than 3 years old when he had a son.

In fact, if these units of time were months instead of years, then the average age of the first 10 patriarchs when they became fathers would have been 13 years old. And the average age of the next 10 would have been 4 years old. Obviously such an explanation would require a series of miracles far greater than that of longevity.

WHY DON'T WE LIVE SO LONG TODAY?

God is the sovereign, omnipotent Creator of the universe. He can do whatever He wishes. To accomplish His purpose, He who made the world by direct fiat, can still perform His will and achieve instant results by merely giving the order. Or, He may choose to work through the natural laws of the universe—which, of course, are laws only because He ordered them into existence. So, no matter how He works, the ultimate cause is still God.

THE OZONE THEORY

In the matter of declining longevity after the Flood, we have a very reasonable explanation of how God might have done it. In his book, *The Biblical Flood and the Ice Epic,* Donald W. Patten, presents an excellent case for the ozone theory.

As most people know, our earth is surrounded by a layer of ozone high in the ionosphere. The Creator placed this protective shield around our planet to filter out deadly shortwave radiation which otherwise would strike our earth.

But since the Flood, earth's planetary wind-system has caused a certain mixing of ozone with our atmosphere, so that as we breathe air, we are also inhaling the deadly gas, ozone.

The mixture is about 2 or 3 parts per million. Insignificant as that may seem, it is undoubtedly a major factor in reducing longevity.

Mr. Patten reports that when ozone experiments were conducted with human guinea pigs, the whole molecular system of the body was thrown into pandemonium directly affecting life itself. It thus becomes apparent that one of the effects of ozone poisoning is aging.

To prove this point, Mr. Patten reports that radiologists who are medical doctors never get in the direct line of the x-rays, for the x-ray equipment produces ozone which they of course breathe for 30 or 40 hours a week. The result is that radiologists have an average life span that is 7 years shorter than that of other doctors. Mr. Patten attributes this reduced life span to their exposure to ozone. Maybe somebody should invent a machine to remove ozone from x-ray rooms and why not from office rooms, living rooms, and bedrooms, too?

In 1971 *Nature Magazine* reported an experiment by a Mr. Setner in which fish were subjected to ozone experimentation. A mixture of oxygen and ozone was injected into the water of the fish tank. The result was a drastic drop in the life span of the fish. When results were plotted with a line graph, the curve matched that of the decline in man's age after the Flood.

Patten concludes that with an increased ozone and carbon dioxide content in our atmosphere, we have a reasonable, scientific explanation for the drop in the longevity of man.

Consider further (1) a thinner ozone shield in the ionosphere allowing more deadly radiation to strike the earth, and (2) a complete radical change in the climate of earth. Put these factors together and we can readily see why man's life span dropped so drastically. And we can understand, too, why animals and trees could not live as long after the Flood as they did before. This will also help to explain why some monstrous birds, reptiles and other animals have become extinct.

After the catastrophe of the Deluge, all life on this planet was locked into a desperate struggle for survival resulting in extinction for some, diminished size for others; but a reduction of life span for all.

7

Did the Flood Really Cover the Whole Earth?

Many people believe it was a local flood, not universal. Each man is entitled to his own opinion, but let such an opinion be based on some evidence, not merely on a man's arbitrary thinking.

There are three reasons that seem conclusive in proving that a flood really did cover the entire earth.

A. WATER DOESN'T STAND IN HEAPS

If the water was deep enough to cover a high mountain in one part of the world, it would certainly have been just as high on the other side of the globe.

Any farm boy who ever played in mud puddles knows that you can't pile up the water in heaps like sand. Water seeks its own level.

The marine fossils on top of Mt. Ararat and other high mountains throughout the world prove that the mountains were once covered with water. This evidence favors a universal flood.

B. IT WOULD HAVE BEEN EASIER TO MIGRATE

Can anyone imagine Noah working so hard for 120 years,

building his big boat in preparation for a local flood? The very thought is ridiculous. All Noah would have had to do would have been to start walking and whistling. Call it migrating.

It certainly would have been a simple matter to migrate to another part of the world. There would have been no need to hand-cut those huge trees and spend so much time at hard labor for 120 years building the monstrous Ark. Doesn't that make sense? It does to me. Just common sense and a little thinking makes one conclude the flood of Noah's time covered the whole earth.

C. AND THAT'S WHAT THE BIBLE SAYS

The previous thoughts were presented for the benefit of those to whom the Bible has not yet become a final, absolute authority. For those to whom it is just that, no other proof is needed than the clear statement of the Word of God.

Genesis 7:19 says, ". . . *all* the high hills, that were under the whole heaven, were covered." Isn't that clear enough? Now, read all of verse 19:

> And the waters prevailed exceedingly upon the earth; and all the high hills, that were under the whole heaven, were covered.

GOD DIDN'T WASTE ANY WATER

While the record clearly indicates it was a universal flood, God didn't waste any water. He made the flood waters just deep enough so the Ark would clear the highest mountain without scraping bottom—no more!

The dimensions of the Ark indicate that while it was floating, the bottom of the barge would have been about 22½ feet below the surface of the water. A shipbuilder told me that. Read verse 20. The waters were 15 cubits above the highest mountain. That would have been about 22½ feet—just enough to allow the Ark to float over the highest mountain without scraping bottom. Isn't it fascinating to observe how carefully God works and how accurately it is all recorded?

In chapter 6, verse 7, we have these words, "And the Lord said, I will destroy man . . . from the face of the earth. . . ."

And in verse 13, notice these words, ". . . behold, I will destroy them with the earth." Note also this verse:

And, behold, I, even I, do bring a flood of waters upon the earth, to destroy all flesh, wherein is the breath of life, from under heaven; and every thing that is in the earth shall die (Gen. 6:17).

And look also at this passage:

For yet seven days, and I will cause it to rain upon the earth forty days and forty nights; and every living substance that I have made will I destroy from off the face of the earth (Gen. 7:4).

Other passages include Genesis 8:21-22; 9:11; and Matthew 24:39. They all clearly speak of a worldwide involvement, not a local situation.

WAS ALL LIFE OUTSIDE THE ARK DESTROYED?

Look again at verses 21 and 22 of chapter 7:

And all flesh died that moved upon the earth, both of fowl, and cattle, and of beasts, and of every creeping thing that creepeth upon the earth, and every man:

All in whose nostrils was the breath of life, of all that was in the dry land, died.

These verses indicate that all life that lived on the dry land and breathed air perished in the Flood—except for the ones Noah took into the Ark. But Noah didn't take any whales, dolphins, fish, or other marine life—just air-breathing, land animals. And, of course, every member of the human race, except for Noah's family of eight, likewise drowned in the awful water-judgment we call the Flood.

That means the giants drowned too. Of course, the demons who lived in them didn't drown. You can't drown demons. As we saw earlier, they were cast into hades, bound and held in darkness, reserved for the final judgment.

One more passage:

Whereby the world that then was, being overflowed with water, perished:

But the heavens and the earth, which are now, by the same word are kept in store, reserved unto fire against the day of judgment and perdition of ungodly men (II Peter 3:6-7).

The Bible clearly tells the story of a flood that covered the whole earth. Who can say it isn't so? The next time it will be a deluge of fire and that will be universal, too. Does anyone think this refers to a "local" fire? I think the evidence is conclusive: the Flood was universal.

8

Where Did All the Water Come From?

Some people think there isn't enough water in the whole world to cover the entire earth. Of course, if this were true, there could not have been a universal flood. Let's look at the evidence.

In the Genesis account of the Flood we are told the flood water came from two sources: the fountains of the great deep and the windows of heaven:

> In the six hundreth year of Noah's life, in the second month, the seventeenth day of the month, the same day were all the fountains of the great deep broken up, and the windows of heaven were opened.

> And the rain was upon the earth forty days and forty nights (Gen. 7:11-12).

"THE WINDOWS OF HEAVEN"

The "windows" were opened, and it rained. The Hebrew word for "window" literally means "sluices." The sluices of heaven were opened. A sluice is a trough. The water literally poured out of the sky. Not gentle rain falling drop by drop, but rather it came down out of "troughs" in a mighty deluge.

But how did all that water get up there in the first place and why had it not rained before? I explained part of that in chapter 3—quoting Genesis 2:6 to show that originally God used a subterranean mist to water the earth instead of rainfall from the sky. But I hasten to say that even though it had not been allowed to fall, there was a great quantity of water high above the sky.

Read carefully Genesis 1:6-7:

> And God said, Let there be a firmament in the midst of the waters, and let it divide the waters from the waters.
> And God made the firmament, and divided the waters which were under the firmament from the waters which were above the firmament: and it was so.

The firmament is what we would ordinarily call the air or the sky. These two verses teach very plainly that God put a lot of water above the sky and a lot of water below the sky so that waters above the firmament were separated from the waters below the firmament.

In verses 9 and 10, God explains more about how He dealt with the second mass of water—that is the waters "under the heaven":

> And God said, Let the waters under the heaven be gathered together unto one place, and let the dry land appear: and it was so.
> And God called the dry land Earth; and the gathering together of the waters called he Seas: and God saw that it was good.

We are told how God separated the land and the water so there was dry land and there were seas or oceans. But nothing more is mentioned in the Bible about those waters above the firmament until Noah starts telling the people that water is going to fall out of the sky. We believe God put the water up there and held it there until He poured it down at the time of the Flood.

THE CANOPY THEORY

Many years ago, Dr. Kellog, a famous scientist and a Christian, suggested that the original earth had a canopy around it. The canopy consisted of moisture high in the stratosphere which, because of the extreme cold, would have been congealed into ice. On more than one occasion, while flying over the ocean at a height of about five miles, I was intrigued by the pilot's announcement, "Outside your window right now the temperature is 40 degrees below zero."

A canopy of ice surrounding planet Earth would have served as the roof on a greenhouse. The heat and light of the sun would have been diffused so that it was not too hot at the equator nor too cold at the poles. The harmful rays of the sun that destroy cells would have been filtered out so the whole earth was a paradise and men could live to be seven, eight, or nine hundred years old.

This will explain how enormous herds of wild animals could be grazing on the north slope of Alaska, which animals were turned into oil as a result of the Flood. Geologists agree that oil is a fossil fuel. It comes from the bodies of animals. Coal comes from trees and plants, but oil comes from animals. To produce all the oil which is under the frozen far-north, there must have been unbelievably huge herds of animals. And that obviously means the climate of the far-north must, at one time, have been favorable for their existence in enormous numbers.

The canopy theory also explains the mammoth mystery of Siberia. Mammoths are now extinct. They were huge animals with trunks and tusks like elephants but much larger. A friend of mine found a mammoth tusk on the bank of the Yukon in Alaska. It was so heavy it took two men to lift it.

Around the turn of the century the body of one of these animals was uncovered in the frozen ice of Siberia. Since then, many have been found. It is amazing that their flesh is so well preserved that dogs will eat the meat. But even more amazing is the fact that in their stomachs are undigested, tropical plants and in their mouths unchewed, unswallowed tropical plants—including buttercups. Even the soft tissue of their eyeballs is well preserved.

With the canopy high in the stratosphere, the whole earth could have enjoyed a delightful temperature. Picture the mammoths grazing in their vast pasturelands of the far-north, feeding leisurely in a semi-tropical paradise.

Suddenly, the canopy collapses and the mammoths are in a state of shock. Water and ice are falling out of the sky. With the "roof of the greenhouse" gone, the sun's rays would come in straight at the equator, shooting the temperature up to an uncomfortable degree. While at the poles, the rays of the sun would be so slanted, the temperature would suddenly take a severe drop—perhaps from 80 degrees above zero to 80 degrees below. Some think the temperature may have dropped to 150 degrees below zero.

The mammoths, with mouths full of grass, would have stopped chewing as they shivered in the frigid temperature that had engulfed them. Within moments they would have been in a deep-freeze, thus to be preserved in solid ice for nearly 5,000 years. Now when the ice of Siberia melts and the bodies of these huge animals are exposed, some of them are still standing in an upright position. Some have one foot partially raised as if in the act of walking when they were frozen before they could lower all their feet. Isn't that incredible! There is no explanation that satisfies me apart from the canopy theory.

WHAT ABOUT THE TILTING OF THE EARTH'S AXIS?

I must say that some evolutionists try to explain the sudden change of temperature in the Arctic Zone by the tilting of the earth's axis. That's a good try but it won't work. Any boy who ever played with a top will see the fallacy of that argument.

It is a law of physics that a spinning gyroscope can change the angle of its axis only very slowly. The earth is a gigantic gyroscope with an axis 8,000 miles long running through the earth from pole to pole. It is spinning at a speed of 1,000 miles an hour at the equator. Now, tell me, how could the earth be tilted on its axis so fast that the mammoths didn't have time to swallow their grass? That's nonsense and any child knows it.

Yes, the axis of the earth did tilt. There is no question about that. But it obviously must have taken some time to make the change. Again, the only reasonable explanation, in my opinion, is that of the Flood.

A universal flood would have meant a tide that had no stopping point—a tide that continued to sweep around the world—possibly gaining height and weight all the while. Some have estimated such a tidal wave could have been several miles high. That would have been sufficient to make the old earth wobble so that eventually the axis of the earth stabilized on the slant as it is today. That makes sense to me.

POST FLOOD CONDITIONS
MADE SURVIVAL MORE DIFFICULT

The canopy theory answers a lot of other questions too. With the "roof of the greenhouse" gone after the Flood, the paradise which was earth was drastically changed from a friendly environment to one that was hostile to earth's creatures including men, animals and plants. Now that it was extremely hot at the equator and awfully cold at the poles, the climate of the earth was subject to enormous changes.

The drastically different temperatures in different parts of the world would have generated severe storms, hurricanes, tornadoes, droughts, local floods, and so forth—all new to planet Earth. Many lush tropical feeding grounds would have disappeared. So it is not surprising that mammoths, dinosaurs, and many other creatures could not long survive these harsh conditions of the earth's new environment. Consequently, many of them became extinct.

Man himself was drastically affected also. His longevity was suddenly cut in half. And that was only the beginning. Noah lived 950 years but his oldest son, Shem, lived only 600. And Shem's son lived only 400. The life span of man continued to drop to 200 and finally down to around 100. (Joseph was 110—where we are today.)

So where did all the water come from? Well, in the first place it came out of the sky as God opened the windows of heaven.

THE FOUNTAINS OF THE GREAT DEEP

In the second place we are told that God broke up the fountains of the great deep. I think this involves great underground water reserves which we call the water table. Remember a mist came out of the ground to water the earth. So there had to be an underground water supply to feed springs for rivers as well as to supply the roots of plants.

But I am sure that this must also include the oceans. When God made them He called them Seas. A famous scientist told me he calculated the quantity of water that lies in the great ocean basins and the volume needed to cover the whole earth. He said that if God raised the ocean floor a mile or two and lowered the mountains a comparable distance, there would have been enough water to cover the earth.

The *National Geographic* of December 1974 has a graphic display of a crack in the floor of the Atlantic running from one end to the other (north and south). Even today hot lava emerges through this thin area of the earth's crust.

The main mass of our planet is a molten mass with a hard crust on top that is only a few miles thick. When that crust breaks through under pressure from below, we have the spectacular display called a volanco. A fountain of red-hot liquid rock bursting from the bowels of the earth and spewing high into a night sky must be one of the most awesome sights that human eyes can ever behold on earth.

Many mountains today are said to be of volcanic origin. Certainly with the gigantic upheavals that must have accompanied and followed the Flood, there must have been the rising of many mountain peaks.

At this point we must ask another question.

WHERE DID ALL THE WATER GO AFTER THE FLOOD?

I think the answer is simple. The Bible says, ". . . the waters were abated" (Gen. 8:3). I believe that God slowly lowered the ocean floors as He simultaneously raised the mountains.

Not only did all the water from the oceans return to their basins but all the water which fell out of the sky had to find a place to go, too. So I think God simply made the oceans deeper than they ever were before and at the same time He made the mountains higher. For the Almighty Creator this would have been no problem at all.

Thus the waters were abated from off the earth and the Ark rested . . . on Mt. Ararat.

It is interesting to me as I travel on our superhighways to see where engineers made great cuts through hills and mountains to build these roads as level as possible. The layers of rock thus exposed are fascinating to observe and think about. There are many colors and varieties of rock. But their most interesting feature is that often they are arranged in well-defined strata, indicating they were once different layers of sediment laid down by water. Sometimes they are horizontal, parallel with the highway, and sometimes they are slanted upward at a steep angle. Sometimes they are nearly vertical. It doesn't take much imagination to fit all this into the picture of the Flood as I described above.

9

How Did All Those Animals Get Down From That Icy Mountain?

This is a reasonable question and one that is asked quite frequently.

Genesis 8:4 says, "And the ark rested . . . upon the mountains of Ararat." The Turkish word is *Agri Dagh*—the mountain of agony. But why does the Bible use the plural word "mountains." Even though from a distance it appears as only one mountain, it has 65 separate peaks. It is much bigger than one would think. Its base covers 500 square miles.

It towers nearly 17,000 feet into the sky. The second highest mountain nearby is Little Ararat with an altitude of only 11,000 feet. The upper reaches of Big Ararat lie buried in 17½ square miles of glacial ice.

Fierce blizzards, hail, lightning, avalanches, and violent storms are common. These are the climatic conditions climbers encounter today when searching for the Ark at an elevation of 13,500 feet where the Ark is believed to be buried in the ice.

So how did Noah get his precious cargo of animal-couples down from the parked Ark without any casualties? If he hadn't succeeded in this some animals would have become extinct im-

Map pinpoints the location of Mt. Ararat, which is in a remote area near the Russian border of Turkey.

mediately and they would have had no purpose being in the Ark in the first place.

I believe the answer lies in the fact that Mt. Ararat, like other high mountains, was not so high when Noah left the Ark. The whole process of lowering oceans and raising mountains must have been a gradual thing. It would seem reasonable to suppose that when Noah's menagerie emerged from the Ark, they had no special difficulty in quickly descending to the plains below. Over the years and centuries that followed, Mt. Ararat could have continued to rise slowly until it reached its present height.

This idea is in keeping with a report from Professor William R. Farrand, of the Artic Institute, to SEARCH in 1970, in which he indicates that "the glacial history of Ararat seems to be limited to the past few centuries." He found no evidence that Ararat had any glaciers before the sixteenth century. He explains that before then, either Ararat was too low to support glaciers or, if there were any, they were covered by recent out-pourings of lava. He states further that the wall of one gorge "was composed of alternating layers of thick lava-flows and volcanic ash deposits. No rock of non-volcanic nature was seen . . . ."

Mt. Ararat is obviously a young mountain. It is, therefore, reasonable to assume that the climate on Mt. Ararat was not immediately as formidable as it is today. After all, tradition says that pilgrimages were made regularly up to the Ark in ancient times.

The local Armenian people, who cannot remember a time when their ancestors did not live in this area, call the area around the mountain Noah's Vineyard.

It is interesting to note that the melting snow of Mt. Ararat is the source of the Euphrates River. It is very likely that Noah built his barge in the lower Euphrates Valley—later called Bab-

Jim Bouck (right) and his Kurdish guide on Mt. Ararat in 1975. Mr. Bouck is assisting the author in showing the film *The Ark of Noah*.

How Did All Those Animals Get Down from That Icy Mountain? □ 63

Infrared photograph taken by satellite from 350 miles up—looking down on Mt. Ararat. The Ark is believed to be in the area indicated by the circle, and the large dark area to the left of the circle is the Ahora Gorge which contains the moving glacier.

ylon and Mesopotamia. If that is correct, then we can say that when he landed, he docked his boat at the other end of the same river—a few hundred miles up stream—to the northwest—on top of the mountain.

At any rate, if God had the power to engineer "Operation Deluge" preserving Noah and the animals in the Ark, we can surely believe that He had no difficulty carrying out "Operation Evacuation." You can be sure they were all safe on the plain at the base of the mountain soon after Noah opened the door. Of course, they did not leave the Ark immediately after it rested on the mountain. They had to wait until the plain below had dried sufficiently.

When we talk about the animals there are several other questions that puzzle people.

HOW DID NOAH CORRAL ALL
THOSE ANIMALS INTO THE ARK?

Did he and his boys chase them, coax them, force them, trap them, guide them, call them, or none of these? Let's see what the Bible says. Look at the seventh chapter of Genesis.

Verse 1 tells us that God told Noah to "*Come . . .* into the ark. . . ." Not go! That tells us where God was. Verse 4 says the rain will start in exactly seven days. Verses 5 and 7 tell us Noah obeyed God instantly. We know he didn't procrastinate because according to verses 13 through 16 we learn that all Noah's family and all the animals entered the Ark in one day: "In the selfsame day entered Noah, and Shem, and Ham, and Japheth. . . . They, and every beast . . . into the ark. . . ."

They surely couldn't have lost much time in a great cowboy-type roundup. As a matter of fact, after Noah was in the Ark (v. 7) we read in verse 9: "There went in two and two *unto Noah* into the ark . . . as God had commanded Noah."

In other words, God went in first. He then said to Noah, "Come." So Noah went in with his family. After Noah was in the Ark, the animals all followed—well, all those that were supposed to be in.

Imagine, from the great herd of mammoths grazing on the plain, all of a sudden, two, a male and a female started for the door of the Ark. Can't you see all the other mammoths wondering what these two were doing? They all looked but they never took one step to follow.

Repeat the picture with lions, giraffes, ostriches, zebras, dinosaurs, deer, dogs, squirrels, various birds, mice, insects, and so on and so forth. They all went in "the selfsame day."

I believe when God said: "Come" to Noah, the specific animals that were scheduled to go in, also found themselves moving at God's bidding. After all, God had made them in the first place. He engineered their creation, He controls their function, their habits and even their mysterious, unerring patterns of migration even when flying from the Antarctic to the Arctic as in the case of the Arctic tern. So why couldn't He also cause them to migrate right into the Ark?

Is that too hard to believe? Think about the wonders of the human body, the mysteries of life in a seed, the marvels of osmosis and metamorphosis—all of these are miracles of the God of creation. So why would He have any problem rounding up animals and herding them two by two and seven by seven into Noah's corral called the Ark?

No matter how you look at it, we are dealing with supernatural power. Let's face it, if you decide you don't believe in miracles, you had better start thinking about what you are going to do if and when Noah's Ark is uncovered and displayed to the world. The evidence indicates that a lot of people will soon be faced with that momentous decision.

DID NOAH FEED THE ANIMALS OR
DID THEY HIBERNATE WHILE IN THE ARK?

Here is another question that invariably comes up. The Bible says that Noah stored food in the Ark for his family and the animals. So obviously he fed them during the Flood:

> And take thou unto thee of all food that is eaten, and thou shalt gather it to thee; and it shall be for food for thee, and *for them* (Gen. 6:21).

If you want to know what they ate, read Genesis 1:29 and 30:

> And God said, Behold, I have given *you every herb* bearing seed, which is upon the face of all the earth, and every tree, in the which is the *fruit* of a tree yielding seed; to you it shall be for meat.
>
> And *to every beast* on the earth, and *to every fowl* of the air, and *to every thing that creepeth* upon the earth, wherein there is life, I have given every *green herb* for meat: and it was so.

It is obvious that men and animals were herbivorous from creation to the Flood. Absolutely none were carnivorous and all animals were tame.

But some people ask: "Is it possible that some or all of the animals may have hibernated at least part of the time? After all, would not the litter problem have been unmanageable—especially for the big animals if they were active during their entire stay in the Ark?"

Of course, it's possible, some may have hibernated part of the time. We do not know. But we do know they did not all hibernate all the time.

As for the litter problem, I do not see any great problem. Years ago when I raised a lot of commercial broilers, I spent a lot of money thoroughly cleaning and disinfecting the broiler house after each flock went to market—every 13 weeks. Then Pennsylvania State College told us that wasn't necessary. I followed their advice and when one flock went to market, instead of taking out the litter and disinfecting the place, we just spread clean wood shavings on top of the old filthy litter and put in the next batch of 20,000 baby chicks. For one year no litter was removed. The chicken house was very crowded with less than one square foot of floor space for each chicken. By the time we did clean out at the end of one year, the litter was about one foot deep, but there was no special problem. The smell of ammonia was very strong but any farmer grows accustomed to that. It's the city people who are concerned about this problem. But city people learn to tolerate the factory fumes, smog, and so forth, which farmers find intolerable.

Now consider Noah. Nothing was crowded. The ceiling was 15 feet high and the capacity of the Ark was sufficient so that animals had spacious stables.

Noah's living quarters were probably on the top floor at the one end of the Ark. Don't forget how long the Ark was. Noah lived farther from some of the animals in the Ark than some farmers' houses are from their barns. Remember the Ark was at least 450 feet long.

Noah was a farmer, and I don't think he had any problem handling the animals during the time he was in the Ark—just over one year.

Of course, there are many details of Noah's experiences which we do not know. But I believe we have reasonable explanations for each problem that presents itself.

10

Could It Ever
Happen Again?

Positively not! There will never be another universal flood.

It must have been a glad day when Noah was told to leave the Ark and take all his animals to start a new life on planet Earth (read Gen. 8:15-19).

The first thing Noah did was to build an altar and offer an animal sacrifice to the Lord. This was the reason he had seven of some of the clean animals. He needed extra ones for sacrifice:

> And Noah builded an altar unto the LORD; and took of every clean beast, and of every clean fowl, and offered burnt offerings on the altar.
>
> And the LORD smelled a sweet savour; and the LORD said in his heart, I will not again curse the ground any more for man's sake; for the imagination of man's heart is evil from his youth; neither will I again smite any more every thing living, as I have done.
>
> While the earth remaineth, seedtime and harvest, and cold and heat, and summer and winter, and day and night shall not cease (Gen. 8:20-22).

Notice the words in verse 21 ". . . neither will I again smite any more every thing living, as I have done."

In chapter 9, verse 11, we read God's clear guarantee:

And I will establish my covenant with you; neither shall all flesh be cut off any more by the waters of a flood: neither shall there any more be a flood to destroy the earth.

Then God put a rainbow in the sky as a token of His promise. Noah had never seen a rainbow before. Now each time it started to rain, he could see that rainbow and not be afraid of another deluge. The bow was God's reminder to men that there would never be another universal flood.

But life for Noah and his family was not the same as before the Flood. Yes, they would begin all over again and they would do as God said: "Be fruitful, and multiply, and replenish the earth" (Gen. 9:1). But Noah's life style was changed drastically.

For one thing, the animals became wild. For the first time they were afraid of man and they fled at his approach. This must have been strange to Noah and his sons:

And the fear of you and the dread of you shall be upon every beast of the earth, and upon every fowl of the air, upon all that moveth upon the earth, and upon all the fishes of the sea; into your hand are they delivered (Gen. 9:2).

No wonder animals were afraid. According to verses 3 and 4, man was now to become carnivorous, but he was forbidden to eat blood:

Every moving thing that liveth shall be meat for you; even as the green herb have I given you all things.

But flesh with the life thereof, which is the blood thereof, shall ye not eat.

Just as God had given man the green herbs to eat, now he also gave man "moving things." Obviously this is a reference to animals. This becomes clear when man is quickly told he shall not eat the blood. Centuries later the law of Moses upheld these same instructions. They ate lambs, goats, quail, and other wild game. Jesus spoke of the feasting on the "fatted calf." But the Jews always drained out the blood.

Perhaps this was God's provision for man's welfare in a new and far more hostile environment. Could it be that the struggle for survival required animal protein to help man overcome the battle with increased cosmic radiation which destroyed human cells at a rate far greater than before the Flood?

At any rate, the harsh environment and hostile climate were to take their toll so that the age of men continued to drop sharply for more than ten generations until it was very close to what we experience today.

CAPITAL PUNISHMENT

God instituted something else that was new: Capital Punishment. God told Noah that since man was made in the image of God, human life was so sacred that if any man took another's life, he should pay for such a terrible crime by forfeiting his own life. Capital punishment for cold-blooded murder is very Biblical and the Bible is careful to explain why.

> Whoso sheddeth man's blood, by man shall his blood be shed: for in the image of God made he man (Gen. 9:6).

Noah lived 350 years after the flood. There were none of those wicked, unbelieving mockers around anymore—just his family with a great many grandchildren and great grandchildren. I'm sure Noah was highly honored as the patriarch of the clan, but unfortunately Noah's life was not all joy. Some of his offspring caused him much grief. Others must have given him great satisfaction.

My study of the Biblical chronology leads me to believe that his oldest son, Shem, lived such a long and honored life that he became Melchisedec, King of Salem, to whom Abraham paid tithes in Geneses 14:18. Shem was 100 years old at the time of the Flood and nearly 500 years old when he was King of Salem (Jerusalem). He died at the age of 600—by far the oldest patriarch at that time. Shem was alive during most of the time Abraham lived. He died only a few decades before Abraham did. In the midst of a wicked world, who but the godly patriarch Shem, revered son of Noah, could possibly qualify as the one to whom Abraham, chosen of God to father a new race, would pay a tithe? This explanation seems quite reasonable to me. Of course, God couldn't name him because he was to be used as a type of Christ in the Book of Hebrews—without father or mother. To have named him as a man would have destroyed that picture. But the King of Salem was a living person and Shem seems to fit the picture as no one else does.

PART II

THE STORY
OF THE
SEARCH

11

What Makes You Think the Ark Is Still Up There?

Does the Bible say it was to be preserved? No, not really—not in so many words. But it may be there by implication.

When Jesus said in Luke 17:26, "And as it was in the days of Noe, so shall it be also in the days of the Son of man," He may have been saying more than meets the eye when casually reading that verse. Maybe there is a meaning that remained hidden until now in order not to destroy the Biblical doctrine of the imminent return of Christ.

ARK TO BE DISPLAYED
BEFORE AN UNBELIEVING WORLD

It is just possible that Jesus was saying (only for the benefit of those who would be alive when it happened) that at the time of His return the Ark would again be on public display to warn the world, just like it was before the Flood. We can't say for certain that He had that in mind but neither can we say that He didn't. The more I meditate on this subject, the more I'm inclined to think that "He who knows the end from the beginning," included a special hidden message that would only be made clear to those who would be alive at the time of His return.

At any rate, history is full of records of people who reported the preservation of the Ark. In the last 120 years nearly 200 individuals claim to have seen it. Even if we discard half of these stories, the evidence is so overwhelming that to rule out the existence of the Ark is to create a whole series of questions for which there are absolutely no reasonable answers. Some of those questions will be asked at the end of this chapter.

If the reader is skeptical, he may take comfort in the fact that up to 1970 no one was more skeptical than the author of this book. I explained why in chapter 5. Now let me explain how and why I suddenly changed my mind. It's no sin to be ignorant, but it is a sin to be willfully ignorant—refusing to believe the facts when proof is presented.

So far we do not have absolute proof, only a lot of evidence that points toward that proof. But the evidence is too great to ignore.

I was conducting a tour with Dr. David Hocking of Long Beach, California. We had around 60 people, many of them from Pastor Hocking's church. Enroute to the Holy Land, we went through the Soviet Union. Our schedule was to take us from Moscow to Cairo, Egypt.

At the last moment, we were notified to appear at the airport very early in the morning—much earlier than our schedule indicated. They didn't tell us why. I was disgusted. When I saw the plane I was even more disgusted. But when one is mad at the Russians, he doesn't tell anybody until he is out of the country. So I refrained from protest. Later I learned that they were using "our" jet to fly soldiers to Egypt and we had to be satisfied with an old propeller plane. One reason I was unhappy about the whole deal was because I knew that instead of a high, fast, smooth, nonstop flight, we would have a slower, lower, rougher ride with a stop-off somewhere for refueling. And that's exactly what happened. And now I'm so very glad it did. I'm sure the Lord in His providence arranged all the details to get me involved in His plan for uncovering the Ark.

The last outpost where our Russian plane could refuel before leaving Soviet territory was Yeravan—very close to the Turkish border. There were many police and they were very strict about "no pictures" and no contact with the crowds of natives that had gathered to see all these "wealthy" Americans parade from the plane into a large waiting room. To them all Americans are millionaires.

These Armenian people were very colorful. In their baggy pants, they looked like something out of the *National Geographic.* I learned later the reason the police were so touchy was because missile fuel was manufactured in this area. Of course, I didn't see anything of that operation.

While we were in the waiting room, waiting to board our plane as soon as it was refueled, a few of us walked out on a small porch. Just then one of the local people slipped by the police and came over to us. Pointing at a lofty snowcapped mountain peak nearby, he said: "That's Mt. Ararat; that's where the prophet Noah landed his big boat. ' I'm so glad my good friend, Dan Craig, was in the group. He was born in Argentina and speaks many languages. He understood the man and immediately translated what he said. I took a long look at that mountain and I have not been the same since.

No pictures were allowed but I took a mental picture which almost seemed to haunt me in the days that followed. I couldn't forget that mountain or the words, "That's Mt. Ararat; that's where the prophet Noah landed his big boat."

I remembered that an organization called Search Foundation had been reported as having sent expeditions up Mt. Ararat and that they were seriously looking for the Ark. Foolish as I thought their project, I nevertheless found myself attempting to call them to see if they really had any evidence.

I got an invitation to come to Washington, D.C., to the house of Dr. Ralph Crawford (now deceased), founder of Search Foundation. My wife and I went. We saw movies of their expeditions. We heard many stories of supposedly eyewitness accounts, and we saw and handled a large piece of ancient hardwood which they had found at an elevation of 13,500 feet. Most amazing was the fact that the wood was soaked with pitch and was black in color.

That was the beginning of my interest. Little did I dream that in a few years they would give me a tiny piece of that rare wood—more rare than moon rocks.

My observation to Dr. Crawford was something like this: "How come somebody doesn't write up this story in an attractive, economical brochure so that a great many people could learn about this?"

Dr. Crawford's simple reply was, "Go to it!" In due time I did, and now a few hundred thousand copies of my brochure *Is It the Ark?* are scattered all over this country and some foreign countries, too. Later I'll relate how this brochure spawned the film—*The Ark of Noah.*

The brochure gives some of the accounts, but now I want to present a more complete resume. This list is by no means complete but it should serve to indicate that a great many people through the centuries have testified to the preservation of the Ark.

Kelly Segraves, on page 76 of his book, *The Great Dinosaur Mistake,* makes the following statement: "In recent times the Ark has been seen by over 186 different people, on 17 different expeditions since 1856." In each case the sighting was on the highest mountain in Asia Minor, called Mt. Ararat—so named by Moses some 4,000 years ago.

THE MEANING OF LOCAL NAMES

It is not surprising that the name "Ararat" means "holy ground." To add to the picture we should state that the Armenian people claim *Naxuana* or *Nakitchevan,* located near the mountain, is the burial place of Noah. The name, they say, means "Here Noah settled." The level plain around the mountain they call "Noah's Vineyard."

Mt. Ararat, in the Persian language, is called *Koh-i-Nuh* or "Noah's Mountain." This lofty mountain is in northeast Turkey—close to the borders of the Soviet Union and Iran.

The ancient name for the area around Mt. Ararat is *Terephaminin,* which is translated "region of the eight." The name of the town of Marand is said to mean "the mother is here." Local tradition says that Noah's wife died shortly after the Flood and was buried in this place.

The Araxes River today forms the border between Russia and

The stationary ice pack in the cove where the Ark is believed to be located. The arrow indicates the crevasse where Mr. Navarra saw 50 tons of timber. The large moving glacier is in the foreground. *(Photo courtesy of Search Foundation)*

Turkey. The melting ice on Mt. Ararat is the source of the Araxes River which today forms the border between Turkey and the Soviet Union. The word Araxes is said to mean "River of the Ark."

The ancient town of Ahora is reported to be the place where Noah planted a vineyard. Local people say vines continued to grow and produce grapes until a mighty earthquake in 1828 destroyed the entire area. The word "Ahora" means "Here he planted the vine."

Another town in the area is Ortulu which means "place of dispersal." It is believed the descendants of Noah began their scattered migrations from this place.

Another village, Kohran means "the village of Noah."

REPORTS OF THE ARK ON ARARAT

1. The earliest account published about 275 B.C. says that Berosus, the Babylonian priest, reported the Ark was still in existence.

2. Josephus, the Jewish historian, writing in the second century A.D., soon after the New Testament was finished, men-

tions the remains of the Ark three times. Here is some of what Josephus wrote in his *Antiquities of the Jews*, Book I, Chapter III:

> ... the Armenians call this place (*Naxuana*) "The Place of Descent"; for the ark being saved in that place, its remains are shewn there by the inhabitants to this day. Now all the writers of barbarian histories make mention of this flood and of this ark; among whom is Berosus the Chaldean; for when he is describing the circumstances of the flood, he goes on thus: "It is said there is still some part of this ship in Armenia, at the mountain of the Cordyeans; and that some people carry off pieces of the bitumen, which they take away and use chiefly as amulets for the averting of mischiefs." Hieronymus the Egyptian, also, who wrote the Phoenician Antiquities, and Mnaseas, and a great many more, make mention of the same.

3. From the *Ante-Nicene Fathers*, we have this quotation credited to Theophilus, Bishop of Antioch, in the latter part of the second century, A.D.:

> Moses showed that the flood lasted forty days and forty nights, torrents pouring from heaven, and from the fountains of the deep breaking up, so that the water overtopped every high hill 15 cubits. And thus the race of all the men that then were was destroyed, and those only who were protected in the ark were saved; and these, we have already said, were eight. And of the ark, the remains are to this day to be seen in the Arabian mountains.

4. In the fourth century, Faustus, in his book, *Historical Library*, tells a very interesting story as part of the history of Armenia. He speaks of a devout bishop called Jacob, who came from Nisibis, a powerful city of ancient Mesopotamia. With great zeal he climbed Mt. Ararat in search of the Ark. When he descended with his companions carrying a piece of the Ark, he found the whole town waiting to greet him. He presented them with the wood which tradition says was later placed in the Monastery of Echmiadzin.

5. Many writers in subsequent centuries talk about the "holy man," Jacob. One such is the monk, Epiphanius of Salamis who, in defending the authority of the Bible, wrote: "Do you seriously suppose that we are unable to prove our point, when even to this day the remains of Noah's Ark are shown in the country of the Kurds?"

6. John Chrysostom, called the greatest preacher of the ancient church, is quoted as saying (near the end of the fourth

century):

> Let us therefore ask them [the unbelieving]: "Have you heard of the Flood—of that universal destruction? That was not just a threat, was it? Did it not really come to pass—was not this mighty work carried out? Do not the mountains of Armenia testify to it, where the Ark rested? And are not the remains of the Ark preserved there to this very day for our admonition?"

7. Isidore of Seville, called one of the most learned men of his time, wrote around the end of the sixth century: "Ararat is a mountain in Armenia, where the historians testify that the Ark came to rest after the Flood. So even to this day wooden remains of it are to be seen there."

8. In the thirteenth century, a medieval scholar, named Vincent, wrote:

> In Armenia there is a noble city called Ani where a thousand churches and a hundred thousand families or households are to be found. The Tartars captured this city in twelve days. Near it is Mount Ararat, where Noah's ark rests, and at the foot of that mountain is the first city which Noah built, called Laudume.

This writer rehearses the story of Jacob, the monk, who brought down a piece of Noah's ark which he says was subsequently placed in a monastery at the foot of the mountain.

9. In 1254 a Flemish explorer, William of Ruysbroeck, after visiting the area, called Mt. Ararat "the mother of the world," and he reported that no man could climb to the top.

10. Around the end of the thirteenth century, Marco Polo visited this area enroute to China. He reported also that no man could reach the top but he said the natives reported to him the Ark of Noah was on the mountain.

11. Also in the thirteenth century, an Armenian prince named Haithon, in writing about the "marvels of the thirteen kingdoms of Asia," speaking of Mt. Ararat, wrote: "On that mountain Noah's Ark landed after the Flood . . . at the summit a great black object is always visible, which is said to be the Ark of Noah."

12. In the middle of the fourteenth century, Pegolotti prepared a handbook of international trade to be used by various merchants engaged in commerce. Indicating the amount of toll to be collected when passing through the area at the base of Ararat, Pegolotti identifies the toll station as being "under

Noah's Ark," indicating that the location of the Ark of Mt. Ararat was common knowledge, even among the international merchants.

13. Sir John Mandeville, an English knight, wrote in the fourteenth century: ". . . and there is another mountain called Ararat, but the Jews call it Taneez, where Noah's ship rested, and still is upon that mountain . . . ."

14. In 1677, Struys, a Dutch traveler, through some very complicated circumstances, found himself in the monastery located on the slopes of Mt. Ararat. One of the monks gave him this, and other testimony in writing: "I, myself, entered the Ark and with my own hands cut from the wood of one of its compartments the fragment from which that cross is made." Signed by Domingo Alessandro of Rome.

15. Aga Hussein, an Arab, was reported to have climbed the mountain and found the remains of the Ark. The report was made in 1800 by C. J. Rich, an American.

16. In 1840, after the explosion that enlarged the Ahora Gorge, Turkish troops were sent up Mt. Ararat to erect barricades to control the avalanches. In the course of their work, they reported seeing an old ship partly covered by the glacier.

17. About the middle of the nineteenth century, three atheistic scientists announced to the world that they would settle the claims about the Ark by climbing Ararat. They hired Armenian guides and started their climb. They were shocked to discover the Ark was really there. They tried to burn it but couldn't. It was too big to destroy by any means at their disposal. So they threatened death to the guides if they revealed the truth and so descended from the mountain to announce to the world that it was as they expected—no Ark!

In 1920 an Armenian named Haji Yearam, died in California. On his deathbed he revealed the story. He and his father were the guides.

18. In 1876, James Bryce, a noted British scholar and member of Parliament, conducted extensive research and then climbed Mt. Ararat. He found a piece of hand-tooled timber four feet long and five inches thick. But he was ridiculed when he tried to convince the Royal Geographic Society that it was a piece of Noah's Ark.

19. The *Chicago Tribune* of August 1883, reports that a group of Turkish engineers, sent up Mt. Ararat to investigate the avalanches, reported finding a huge carcass of a barge protruding from the glacier. They were said to have found rooms inside.

20. Toward the end of the nineteenth century we have a very interesting account pertaining to the episcopal head of the Nestorian Church of Malabar, South India, Archdeacon Nouri. He was a learned man eloquent in 13 languages. He traveled Europe, Africa, China, Australia, and America and is said to have visited most of the rulers of those lands.

In 1893 he attended the World's Parliament of Religions held in Chicago. He reported to the people there that he had seen Noah's Ark. He said he made three attempts to climb Mt. Ararat before he finally succeeded.

He said he stood overwhelmed and awed as he saw the old Ark there—wedged in the rocks and half filled with snow and ice. He reported that he was inside and that the measurements coincided exactly with the Biblical account.

There was great interest on the part of individuals, but unfortunately, the officials apparently did not take him too seriously. He tried to organize an expedition to the mountain but failed.

21. George Hagopian, an Armenian, born in 1891, went with his uncle on two occasions up the slopes of Mt. Ararat to see the Ark—1902 and 1904. He fled to America in 1913 after the Turks overran his native land—slaughtering many Armenian Christians. He became an American citizen in 1927. He was a carpenter at first but later became a rug dealer. He lived in Royal Oak, Maryland—died in Baltimore, and was buried in 1972 in Easton, Maryland.

At age 78, Mr. Hagopian was interviewed by the late Dr. Crawford of Search Foundation. He was convinced that, as a boy, he had twice seen and entered Noah's Ark.

22. In 1916 two Russian flyers flew over Mt. Ararat and reported seeing a huge ancient ship high on the slopes of Ararat. Their commanding officer took a look for himself. The result was an order from the Czar that sent 150 men on an expedition. They found the Ark, explored it, took measurements and pictures. In the meantime, the communist revolution of 1917 took

place. The Czar was killed and presumably the records were destroyed.

The main pilot, Roshovitsky, escaped to America where he died a few years ago. He told the story and it was reported in an article called: "Noah's Ark Found."

The general who was the commanding officer also came to America. Dr. Crawford talked with him in San Francisco in 1962 when he was 92 years old. He was a tall man (about 6 feet, 6 inches). His mind was a bit hazy concerning the present but seemed clear when talking about the past. He was sure they had seen Noah's Ark.

23. In 1933 Carveth Wells, an explorer and radio commentator, visited the area just inside the Russian border, especially the monastery at Echmiadzin. The monks there displayed a large piece of wood they claimed had been brought down from the Ark.

24. In 1936 Hardwicke Knight, a New Zealand archaeologist, in scouting the mountain, inadvertantly came upon some huge ancient timbers but did not realize until later that he may actually have seen part of the Ark.

25. Dr. Liedmann, a Swedish neurosurgeon whose parents had migrated from the Russian Ukraine, was shown a set of three pictures by a friend who was a major in the Soviet Airforce. They met in Germany in 1947. The pictures showed a Soviet plane in the air over an icecapped mountain and each picture showed a boat-like structure which the Russian major pointed out as being Noah's Ark. The pictures were taken in 1938. The officer said they were going there each year because there were only about 30 to 38 days in the year when weather was favorable for picture taking.

In 1948 they met again and the Russian officer showed Dr. Liedmann a new set of pictures taken "since I saw you a year ago."

Dr. Liedmann reported that in the first set of pictures taken in 1938, a large section of the Ark was exposed. But in the second set most of it was covered with ice. They met again a third time but there were other Russians present and the major pretended to know nothing about the subject.

Said Dr. Liedmann, ". . . I believe absolutely that Noah's Ark was there." The full report is given with a sketch by Dr. Lied-mann on pages 329-333 in Violet Cumming's book, *Noah's Ark: Fact or Fable.*

26. In 1948 a Kurdish farmer, named Reshit, reported that he and others of his clan had seen the Ark. He describes the wood as being "dark and very hard."

27. In 1953 George Greene, an American geologist working for an oil company, flew over Mt. Ararat in a helicopter. He saw the Ark and took many pictures which he showed to a number of his friends. He failed in trying to raise money for an expedition, so he headed for South America hoping to find a fortune there. He took his pictures with him. Bandits killed him and his pictures disappeared. Many individuals testify to the fact that they could clearly see the Ark in the pictures, but not a single picture can be found today.

28. In 1952 Mr. Navarra, French industrialist and mountain climber, scaled Mt. Ararat but found nothing. He climbed again in 1953 and again he found nothing. But he didn't give up. He had inside information from an Armenian friend who claimed his grandfather had seen the Ark and had given him a map pinpointing the location.

So Fernand Navarra and his 12-year-old son, Raphael, climbed in 1955 to produce what is the best evidence we have to date.

In a crevasse, 35 feet down, they found a huge mass of black, hand-tooled timber. Mr. Navarra chopped into the ice to get to the treasure. He touched the wood and exclaimed, "I have touched Noah's Ark." He brought back a large piece of hardwood saturated with bituminous preservative.

29. In 1969 Navarra accompanied an expedition of Search Foundation, headed by the late Bud Crawford, to the same site and they found additional pieces of the same wood.

Many other expeditions have climbed Mt. Ararat since 1969 but up to now the mountain has clutched its treasure, keeping it hidden in its icy bosom—waiting for the right moment. Up to now, that moment has not come.

But who can say there is nothing there when the evidence is so persuasive. Even if half of the above accounts were discarded, we would still have evidence that needs to be reckoned with.

The late Dr. Ralph Crawford, founding president of Search Foundation, holding a piece of timber and sea salt found on Mt. Ararat.

Left to right: Climbers Bud Crawford, Fernand Navarra and Artic Institute representative Ralph Linton examine the icy crevasse where Mr. Navarra saw 50 tons of timber, 35 feet down into the ice. *(Photo Courtesy of Search Foundation)*

IF THE ARK IS NOT THERE,
THE FOLLOWING QUESTIONS HAVE NO ANSWERS

How can we explain all the recorded testimonies through the last several thousand years telling us it is there?

How did all that timber (Mr. Navarra estimated he saw 50 tons of it) get up there on the mountain at an almost inaccessible height of 13,500 feet—along with a lot of sea salt and marine fossils? The wood is all hardwood and there are no hardwood trees growing within a few hundred miles of the mountain.

Why is all the wood that has been found saturated with pitch?

Why do the native Armenians insist that there never has been a time when they did not know the Ark was still up there?

How can we explain a single log that Mr. Navarra saw in the ice which was 150 feet long, since hardwood trees don't grow that tall anymore? To those who say the wood may have been an old monastery or a shrine built long after the Flood to mark the location of the Ark, we must ask: "Why don't local traditions which go back 4,000 years know about it?" There is not one single record of a monastery high on Mt. Ararat. And who ever heard of a monastery (or shrine) completely soaked with pitch? And how did the monks ever get logs 150 feet long up that tremendously difficult and dangerous mountain? The moving pictures of the various expeditions would indicate that people who make such suggestions are just not familiar with Mt. Ararat.

So the big question remains: IF IT IS NOT THE ARK, WHAT IS IT? Without the Ark, we have no answers. With the Ark, we have no questions.

12

What Difference
Does It Make Anyway?

What difference does it make? It makes all the difference in the world if it induces people to believe and be ready. What difference did it make to the people of Noah's day? It made the difference of life and death, not only for time but for eternity, too.

Use your imagination. Watch the crowds mocking and scoffing as they see the parade of animals follow Noah into the Ark. Finally Noah was in the Ark and so were all the animals (the ones with "reservations"). But there was no water. How foolish that must have made Noah appear in the eyes of the people to whom he had preached so long! Can't you hear them calling out, "OK Noah. Let's see it rain." But nothing happened. It reminds us of the treatment Jesus got on the cross when He was challenged by the mocking priests to come down from the cross and prove His deity. Today the crowds mock and scoff at the second coming of Christ just as Peter said they would do and just as they did in Noah's day.

Well, I'm sure the crowds outside the Ark took advantage of the situation and ridiculed poor, old Noah. But Noah wasn't worried. I'm sure he was very sad as he contemplated their fate, but he wasn't worried. God had told him there would be exactly seven days before the rain would start.

He had done all he could; they would not listen; they would not believe. Several days passed and still no rain. But Noah knew that everything was on schedule.

He needed this time to get organized for doing all the chores involved with caring for the animals. He also needed to become accustomed to housekeeping in their new houseboat before they actually set sail in the storm. So I'm sure Noah and his family had plenty to do feeding the animals and arranging affairs in their new living quarters.

FINALLY DAY SEVEN DAWNED

It must have been a beautiful day as every day had been since creation. People were going about their daily activities like meals, weddings, honeymoons, and so on, perhaps ignoring Noah now, having tired of their mockery.

Imagine, then, this scene: Suddenly, without warning, there was a terrible bolt of lightning that brought panic to the whole paradise. Simultaneously solid sheets of water fell from a darkened sky. Loud, frightening roars of thunder seemed to shake the earth. Nobody had ever heard or seen anything like that before. But every human being knew the awful truth: NOAH WAS RIGHT! BUT IT WAS NOW TOO LATE! What sad words! TOO LATE!

We live late in the twentieth century. We have the warning of Jesus telling us that as it was in the days of Noah, so it will be when Jesus comes again:

> And as it was in the days of Noe, so shall it be also in the days of the Son of man (Luke 17:26).

But the crowds don't believe in Noah. They call his story the number one fable of the Bible. So, of course, they do not believe in the second coming of Christ either. Many of us feel certain that the return of Christ to this earth is going to happen soon. The record of Bible prophecy and current events convinces us that this great event is near. But most people think that is foolish and superstitious. Of course, they are only demonstrating what they have been taught, directly or indirectly, by the God-is-dead theologians and by college professors who have decided to reject the Bible as God's Word. They have rejected the Biblical creation story in favor of the evolutionary hypothesis because they are not willing to accept the miracle of instant creation.

Likewise, they have rejected God's account of how sin entered the human race and the story of God's judgment. The real reason for this is that "men love darkness rather than light." That is to say, they love their sin and they hate the idea of God's judgment for sin. So they simply reject the whole story of the "fall" of man. By the time one has covered the story of *creation* and the *fall* in the Book of Genesis, he comes to the story of Noah—which is more of the same—sin and judgment. So he throws this out, too.

An illustration of how the early chapters of Genesis are explained by such men is given in the following quotation from the classroom lecture notes of a college professor in a course in religion in a so-called Christian college in the Midwest.

LECTURE ON GENESIS I-II

"I. The first thing we need to know is that this material is folk literature. This means that it is not simply the product of one individual writer. Instead it is the end result of a long process of storytelling. In literary form most of these stories are legends. . . . Thus we must look at these stories as parables.

"II. The second thing we need to know is that Genesis I-II is really a whole series of legends which had little relation to one another at first. The authors of Genesis have taken these various stories and strung them together. . . ."

With professors in so-called Christian colleges teaching young people such nonsense, it is no wonder so many college students reject the Bible. And many pastors are giving their people the same kind of false teaching.

PASTOR QUESTIONS VALIDITY OF BIBLE HISTORY

A pastor with a degree from a well-known graduate school of theology is quoted with the above big headlines in an Ohio newspaper: "I think the people are stretching things pretty far if they think they've found the Ark," explained Rev. ——. He is further quoted as saying that Biblical history was not recorded until long after the Old Testament period, and thus was "merely a collection of campfire meetings handed down through the years and finally recorded." With such a theological bias it is not surprising to find him saying further, "I do not hold the fundamental view that Christ is the only way to God."

What will this preacher say when the Ark is uncovered? And what do the words of Jesus mean when He said, "I am the way, the truth, and the life: no man cometh unto the Father, but by me"? Christ clearly claimed to be the only way to God.

TALK SHOW EXPERIENCE

On one occasion I was participating in a call-in talk-show in Indianapolis. I spoke about the search for the Ark and the Biblical implications. Then it was time for the open-mike calls to come. Many people called with a lot of honest questions, and I was happy to answer most of them at least. But one caller didn't have a question. Rather he gave a lecture. It went something like this:

"Religion has always been associated with one hoax after another and I'm sure this is just one more. . . . I wouldn't be surprised if you fellows took that wood up on Mt. Ararat and hid it there. Then later you went up and said, 'Look what we found. . . .' " Then he hung up.

The announcer turned to me and said, "What do you say to that?"

My answer was, "Isn't it good this is a free country and each person is entitled to his own opinion?"

After we were off the air, I said to the interviewer, "I wouldn't be surprised if that unhappy caller was a preacher who has denied the Bible and is now afraid that his whole life's work will be undone."

"Oh, I know who he was," he replied quickly. "He's the pastor of the —— Church in the suburbs of the city. He calls in frequently and I recognized his voice."

The majority of the preachers emerging from seminary halls to fill the pulpits of America today have been taught to reject the actual historicity of the early chapters of Genesis.

Now, in view of all this, suppose the Ark is uncovered and

displayed to the world so that people will know that the whole story of Noah (in Gen. 5 through 10) is really true. What a tremendous impact! I think it would shatter the theology of the preachers and professors who deny the miracles of the Bible. The impact, I think, would be utterly devastating. They would be forced to face the facts with all their implications or deliberately choose to remain willfully ignorant. This will help explain why all the power of satanic forces seems arrayed against all efforts to uncover the Ark.

The discovery of the Ark, in presenting proof of the early Biblical chapters, would rock the scientific world and pull the rug from under the whole atheistic foundation of communistic ideology. Their whole system is based on atheism—there is no God and the Bible is not true. I'm sure this is one reason why the Soviet leaders are so strongly opposed to any expeditions on Mt. Ararat.

IMPACT ON COLLEGE STUDENTS

So, would it make any difference? I think it would make a profound difference to a great many people. I think the greatest effect would be upon college students who are honestly looking for truth. Up to now, they have been brainwashed by their professors who teach evolution. But if the Ark were uncovered, those who are honest enough to think for themselves would have to reach the conclusion that their professors were wrong. At that point I think many of them would start reading their Bibles and when that happens, some of them at least will find the truth.

Of course, I am aware of the fact that the Bible does not predict a universal turning to faith in God at the end of the age. It does teach that the vast multitudes will reject Christ (Matt. 7:13-14) even as they did when He was here. At any rate, the discovery of the Ark would leave them all "without excuse" at His coming. They couldn't say, "But Lord, we didn't know. We were taught the Bible isn't true."

However, many are already turning from sin to salvation through faith in Christ. I think there will be a great many more after the Ark is uncovered. One man told me that he didn't believe in God or the Bible. He thought "when you're dead, you're dead." Then a friend of his gave him a copy of my brochure on the Ark. The man told me afterward, "I read your brochure and I got nervous. I was afraid I was wrong. And if I was wrong, what a terrible price to pay! So I accepted Christ as my Saviour. Now I'm saved and I am happy. I just want to thank you for writing that brochure."

If one brochure can do that, imagine the impact when the whole Ark is displayed on television and in newspapers, magazines, and books all over the world.

Of course, the Bible teaches we are saved by faith not by sight. There is no question about that. But we already have many great archaeological findings to strengthen our faith. Why not one more? The biggest of all!

After all, we are not talking about seeing the gates of pearl or the streets of gold. We are talking about a ship mentioned in the Bible. I see no conflict with the concept of salvation by faith. I see only a situation where God would make it easier for honest doubters, like Thomas, to become believers by presenting additional evidence to add to a great body of evidence supplied heretofore by God. And it would, I believe, **force people everywhere to make a decision**—a decision that could well involve their eternal destiny.

Dr. Grosvenor, the late editor of the *National Geographic* magazine, made the statement that if the Ark of Noah is ever uncovered, it will be the greatest archaeological discovery of all history.

So what difference does it make? Plenty!

13

Does Anybody Know Exactly Where the Ark Is?

We think so. Look at the picture (next page) of the long slope of the Parott Glacier. See the white spur off to the left. That is a stationary ice pack in a cove, locked in position by rocky ridges at the 13,800 foot level.

The glacier is constantly moving. It slides down the mountain and melts at the 10,000 to 11,000 foot level. But the ice at the top is always being replaced by the elements of the weather. So the glacier never disappears.

On the other hand, the ice in the cove cannot move because it is held in position by the ridges of rocks. This is very important. If the Ark had landed on the glacier it would have been carried down the mountain long ago. But if it is located in the cove, then it remains just where God originally parked it as the flood waters receded.

Imagine a worldwide endless sea with the Ark floating help-lessly—completely at the mercy of the God of heaven! Then imagine that God ordered the Ark to hover over the exact spot He had prepared to park it. As the waters receded, the Ark finally came to rest in the place where God wanted it.

Aerial photo of the large moving glacier, and the stationary cove (indicated by arrow) where the Ark is believed to be located.

Noah and his cargo left the Ark and descended to the plain. He had no further need of his ship. But in the centuries that followed, surely his grandchildren and great-grandchildren would say, "Grandpa, will you take us up to see the Ark?" (Any grandpas who read this will have no trouble visualizing that scene.) And local tradition says that for hundreds of years after the Flood, people made pilgrimages up the mountain to see the Ark and worship Noah's God.

The Ark was soaked with pitch so it wouldn't rot. Thus it was preserved. But in the many centuries that followed, God changed both the height of the mountain and the weather so that the Ark was buried in ice and snow most of the time. Thus it was no longer easily accessible, and most of the world entirely forgot about it.

But does anybody really know where it is? We think it is in the cove, frozen in a huge block of ice. After all, that's where Mr. Navarra went down 35 feet into a crevasse and saw 50 tons of timber soaked with pitch.

In 1969 Search Foundation found more pieces of black timber just a short distance down the slope in the place where the melting ice water flowed from the cove. These pieces were all small, less than a cubit in length, and probably broke loose from the Ark and floated down to the place where they were found.

But, the 50 tons of timber, it would seem, must mark the location of the Ark itself. That would mean that the Ark is in the cove. Now compare these dimensions. The Ark is 450 to 500 feet long; the cove is about 600 feet long. The Ark is 75 feet wide; the cove is about 150 feet wide. The Ark is 45 feet high; the cove is estimated to be 75 to 100 feet deep. That would mean the Ark has about 35 or 40 feet of ice on top of it.

Observe that the Ark would have fitted into the spot God prepared for it like a car fits in a garage. But, of course, the Ark entered its parking spot by settling from above. So, we believe, there it rests—pitched and parked by God's command—waiting for the big moment when God will order it to be unveiled before the world.

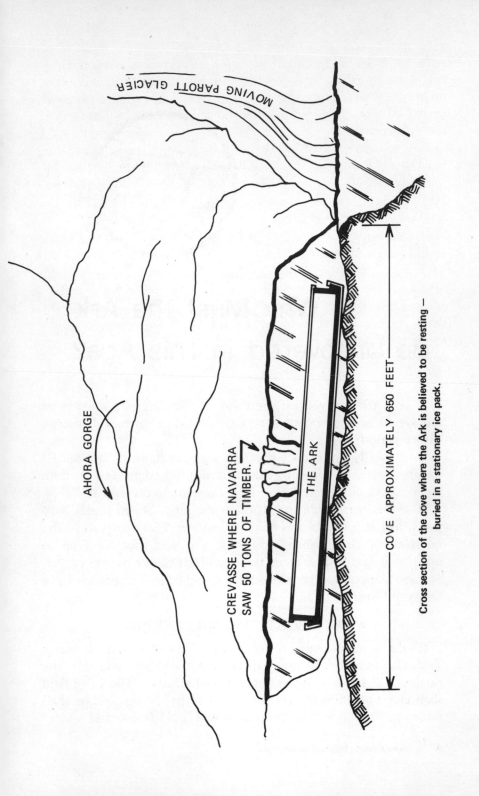

MOVING PAROTT GLACIER

AHORA GORGE

CREVASSE WHERE NAVARRA
SAW 50 TONS OF TIMBER.

THE ARK

COVE APPROXIMATELY 650 FEET

Cross section of the cove where the Ark is believed to be resting —
buried in a stationary ice pack.

14

Why Must the Ark
Be Uncovered in This Age?

If the Ark really is up there on Mt. Ararat, why must it be uncovered in this present age? Could God be saving it for some future period?

God told Noah to coat the Ark with pitch, inside and out. If we are correct in assuming that God did this to preserve it, then we must ask ourselves, "Why did God want to preserve it?"

It seems reasonable that the answer must be: to reveal it to the world at a special moment in history. That brings us to the question of time. **When** would be the best time for God to uncover it and display it to the world? It hasn't happened yet. So God's appointed time must be ahead of us, not behind us in terms of history.

WHAT ABOUT THE MILLENNIUM?

Could it be during the 1000-year reign of Christ of which Zechariah says, ". . . the Lord shall be king over all the earth . . . ." Luke wrote at the birth of Christ: "The Lord God shall give unto him the throne of his father David: and he shall reign . . . ." John tells us the period will last 1,000 years.

Is God preserving the Ark to be exposed during that time? Hardly! It would seem that if the Lord Himself is here in person as many Scriptures teach, nothing would be added by exposing the old wooden barge which Noah used. The presence of the Ark would be nothing compared with the presence of the King of kings. So I believe we must conclude that He preserved it for another period.

OR PERHAPS THE GREAT TRIBULATION?

What about that day of which Jesus spoke when He said, "For then shall be great tribulation, such as was not since the beginning of the world to this time, no, nor ever shall be"? Could God be saving the Ark for the Great Tribulation period? In the Book of Revelation, John tells us that during this period God will send two supernatural witnesses who will prophesy and perform miracles. They will spit fire, devouring their enemies; they will close the rain clouds; change water to blood; and command plagues to torment people on the earth. All this sounds to me like Moses and Elijah—the head of the law and the head of the prophets in Old Testament times.

With Moses and Elijah (or whoever they may be) here on earth performing miracles like that, the news of the discovery of Noah's Ark would be relegated to a small paragraph on page 10. So we must conclude that God did not preserve the Ark for the Great Tribulation period.

So where does that leave us but right here and now during this present age? That's the only time that is left. Since this age will end with the coming of the Lord, it seems perfectly obvious that if God preserved it, His purpose was to reveal it in the last days of the Church Age or Age of Grace. NOW! We cannot say that the Lord cannot come before the Ark is revealed, but we can say that if the Ark is revealed, and the Lord has not yet come, then everybody will have had his final warning, and we will know that the end is near.

WHAT IF YOU ARE WRONG?

A man once said to me, "Aren't you sticking your neck out pretty far? What will you do if they uncover the artifact and find out it wasn't Noah's Ark after all?"

My answer to that was very simple, "I'll just say, 'I was wrong.' After all, that won't change the history of the Flood one iota."

Then I directed a question to him, "What will you do if it is Noah's Ark?" He wouldn't give me an answer. I have found that response to be typical of individuals who decided ahead of time that they will not believe what they don't want to believe—even when the proof is presented.

15

Why Not an Expedition Now?

Why don't we send a big expedition up there and settle the whole question once and for all? Can't we get the U. S. Government, the Turkish Government, the *National Geographic*, and so forth, all together and get some action?

The answer is that governments shy away from offending the Russians. Mt. Ararat is near the border of the Soviet Union and has been declared a military zone. Turkish soldiers are stationed there all the time. Officially, therefore, no foreigners are allowed on the mountain—especially not Americans.

HERE ARE SOME OF THE REASONS

The Turkish Government is Moslem. Their holy book, the Koran, tells them the Ark is on another mountain. They aren't interested in helping prove the Koran wrong. Bart LaRue has an explanation that may help them avoid embarrassment. He says the name used in the Koran really differs only in one letter and it may be that a scribe for Mohammed was responsible for an error in copying the manuscript. In due time complete Turkish cooperation is expected. It could be very soon.

Secular organizations staffed by men who don't believe the

Biblical record are not interested in stirring the intellectual waters and rocking the boat of evolutionary teaching. And pastors who reject the historicity of the Bible likewise are not interested in helping prove themselves wrong and thus upsetting their own theological apple cart. So there are many people who by their deliberate decision simply are not interested at all.

Up to now, it should be stated, most people who have been involved are individuals who believe the Bible. Others often consider the matter foolish because they are not willing to consider the implications. They promptly dismiss the whole matter without even seriously considering the evidence.

But things are happening and by the time the film, *The Ark of Noah*, has been shown all over the free world, it may well be that a big expedition with full Turkish Government cooperation, may become a reality.

There is also a possibility that an expedition will not even be needed at all. We have assumed that is what it would take but maybe God has other plans. How about a little earthquake?

The day after I first mentioned this possibility publicly, a lady gave me a newspaper clipping with the following account.

In the April 18, 1976, edition of the *Grit* is a picture of mourning mothers at the base of Mt. Ararat, looking at the bodies of three children killed in an earthquake. Under the picture the caption says: "TURKEY: Mothers weep over children who were injured during an earthquake at Dogubayazit, a village near Mount Ararat in the Armenian region of Eastern Turkey."

Turkey has many earthquakes. God might use one more to expose Ararat's treasure.

EXPEDITION OR EARTHQUAKE?
GOD WILL SELECT METHOD

The One who holds the whole world in His hands also holds the key that will unlock the Ark and expose it to the world of whom He will then demand a decision.

He may permit a full-scale expedition to fly up to the 13,800 foot level with Turkish Army helicopters, magnesium torches to slice the ice, and bulldozers to shove the ice out of the cove, thus exposing the artifact. Even as I write this manuscript, negotiations are taking place with high Turkish officials and plans are being made. This could well happen in the next year or two. This is what we expect.

Or God might simply order an earthquake to split the rocky ridge and release the gigantic ice pack which we believe is holding the Ark in its icy bosom high on the rim of the Ahora Gorge. This huge block of ice is about 600 feet long, 150 feet wide and maybe 100 feet deep, more or less.

If God ordered an earthquake to release the ice pack, it is conceivable that the huge block of ice might go sliding down the steep slope of the mountain like an enormous ice cube— carrying the Ark with it. In that case, the whole thing could be photographed and published to the world within a few days. No Turkish permit would be needed. And the Russians couldn't do anything about it.

In a relatively few hours, photographers from all over the world could be on the scene taking pictures. Undoubtedly the ice would crack and crumble to pieces as the mighty avalanche tobogganed down the steep slope of the mountain. The Ark itself could be severely damaged. But that would make no difference as long as it could be recognized as having been an ancient barge about 450 feet long—made of tar-soaked timber— that's all it would take to prove its identity as the Ark of Noah. Remember all this could happen overnight.

GOD ALSO SELECTS THE TIME

Whatever method God elects to use to expose the Ark, we can be sure He has also selected the precise moment in history which best suits His sovereign will and purpose.

GOD IS SOVEREIGN

Make no mistake about it, God is very much alive and He is on the throne. He not only holds the whole world in His hands, but He runs it. Although He tolerates temporarily the wicked shinnanigans of mortals, nevertheless He "worketh all things after the counsel of his own will." Paul said that in Ephesians 1:11.

The first great monarch of Babylon, Nebuchadnezzar, in speaking of the God of Daniel, said: "And all the inhabitants of the earth are reputed as nothing: and he doeth according to his will in the army of heaven, and among the inhabitants of the earth: and none can stay his hand . . ." (Dan. 4:35).

We may not see the hand of God in the fabric of history, but that only betrays our poor spiritual vision. Those who have eyes to see can clearly identify the fingerprints of God on the latticework of time. Nothing can happen but what He allows, and in the final outcome His sovereign will will triumph.

One day in 1970 the late Dr. Ralph Crawford, founding president of Search Foundation, sat down to write an article on this subject as he was writing a book review. Here is part of what he wrote.

> If life, with its perplexities, is an enigma to you; if the current scene seems to have no apparent pattern, but rather a bewildering complexity of unrelated tragedies; if some great sorrow, disappointment, or dire perplexity has turned your whole world blank, and it is hard for you to believe the teaching of Romans 8:28, or that God is still in control—then you owe it to yourself to read as quickly as you can this masterpiece of thought and good writing. These are measured words. This book will give vastly needed help to even those who cherish a belief in a loving God.
>
> There is an ever-growing tendency in nearly every heart to conclude that, although right will finally triumph, evil is presently in command. But the fact is that God has never for a moment lost control. Even in the darkness He is silently and inexorably working out the purposes of His will.
>
> . . . There is nothing haphazard in such a life, nothing accidental. God's people move in a chosen pathway, step by step. God makes no experiments with them; they are not pawns on a chessboard, by the moving of which, God may win or lose. Every move is arranged.

He had scarcely finished the article when the telephone rang. It was his daughter-in-law informing him of the instant death of his only son, Harry "Bud" Crawford, in a head-on collision near his home in Denver, Colorado. Bud had been the leader of seven Search Expeditions up the dangerous slopes of Mt. Ararat. He was the only American to stand seven times on the very top of this forbidding mountain. How could it be that he should have escaped all the fierce rigors and death-thrusts of Ararat, only to die in an automobile accident at home!

When Dr. Crawford hung up the receiver, he picked up his manuscript and read what he had just written, taking comfort for his own sorrowing heart. His comment to me later was: "I read it for myself and I didn't change a word."

Concerning the time for the uncovering of the Ark, Dr. Crawford said, "God is sovereign. When His time comes, He will open the door. We just want to be ready to walk in."

16

So What Is the Present Situation?

This question has already been answered in part. Things are happening behind the scenes. Plans are being made. But God still rules and overrules in the affairs of men. Sometimes He "works in mysterious ways, his wonders to perform."

In the past, Dr. Crawford liked to remind me, "Brother, the Lord brought us together." Well, I'm sure that's true and I've already told you how that happened.

Now let me relate another providential arrangement of circumstances with vast repercussions.

BROCHURE INSPIRES A FILM

Dr. Crawford gave a copy of my brochure, *Is It the Ark?* to his friend, Texas oil man Jack Grimm. Jack Grimm in turn gave it to his friend, Hollywood movie producer Bart LaRue. Bart told me later, "When I read your brochure I was floored; I never heard anything like that."

The result was that Jack Grimm and Bart LaRue decided to team-up and produce a movie telling to the world the whole story of the Flood and the search for the Ark.

In the summer of 1974, Bart made a daring climb up Ararat's

treacherous slopes to get the pictures he needed of the mountain. In the film he tells the Bible story, presents archaeological evidence, stone-tablet inscription translations, and so forth. He also incorporated film supplied by Search Foundation showing expeditions on the mountain, including pictures of Mr. Navarra finding a lot of wood deep in an icy crevasse.

Mr. Navarra and the late Dr. Crawford both appear in the film which is a professional documentary, nearly two hours in length. It is currently being shown in theaters all over the United States. Soon it will go to foreign countries and all over the free world.

While this manuscript was being finished, I received word that a copy of the film was being airmailed to me to show in churches or other places of my choosing. The latest report as this book goes to press is that eager audiences overflow many churches to see the film. Many times people are being turned away because the auditorium cannot hold everybody who comes to see the picture. Expressions of gratitude follow in abundance. Requests for showing the film are pouring in from all over the country. People want to see it and most of those who do, are thrilled. Quite a few have already accepted Christ as a result of viewing this film. All of this is a tremendous source of satisfaction to this author.

It is believed that in due time various factors, including this film, will cause world opinion to be so strong in demanding an expedition that neither the Russians nor the Turks will feel comfortable in denying such an expedition. And maybe, at this point, we'll get some action. At any rate, it is a fascinating film, receiving a tremendous reception wherever it is shown and I'm sure its world impact will be substantial.

SIDE EFFECTS AND FRINGE BENEFITS

Early in 1976 Bart LaRue arrived at a Texas radio station to plug his film. The station manager told him, "I have a problem. Madalyn O'Hair is in the studio waiting to debate a Baptist preacher who hasn't arrived. It's time to go on the air. Will you go in and talk to her?"

Bart's answer was, "Not me!" But to help the station manager out of his predicament, Bart went. He told me Madalyn poured out her usual "venom" against Catholics, Baptists, so on and so forth.

Bart finally stopped her. He said, "Wait a minute. You are not talking to me. I don't belong to any of those groups. I'm just a Hollywood producer who recently came to believe that the Bible is true. I just finished a film called *The Ark of Noah*. I made 200 films but this one changed my life. So let's talk about what I know."

So Bart proceeded to tell her how he made the film. He presented the archaeological evidence for the Flood and the historical evidence for the Ark's present existence.

As I listened to Bart tell the story, I got the impression that Madalyn was somewhat thrown off guard, not knowing quite what to say. After all, how could one argue with what Bart was reporting.

Finally, Bart turned to Madalyn's son, who was also present, and said: "If we can uncover Noah's Ark and prove that the early chapters of Genesis are true, *will you become a Christian?*"

And what do you think he said? His answer was, "Yes." On the air, he committed himself. Isn't that fantastic? He was the boy for whom his mother wanted no prayer in school.

At that point Bart turned to Madalyn and said, "What about you?"

And Madalyn said, "No!"

Bart told me, "I really let her have it. I said, 'You are a hypocrite; you're a phoney. You say that even if we prove it, you won't believe it.' "

A few months later an announcement in the newspaper reported that Mrs. O'Hair had resigned as head of world atheism. It would be interesting to know how much her encounter with Bart LaRue had to do with that humiliating decision. Could it be that even she was shaken by the evidence?

It was reported in the newspaper that she claimed the Christians abused her, the atheists did not support her, her own family did not support her, no one supported her. The article quoted her as saying, "They can have it; I quit."

WE MUST BE PATIENT

The present situation is pregnant with potential and our expectations are great. Negotiations are proceeding quietly behind the scenes. I have been told that relations with the Turks have never been better. The whole situation seems to be building up toward a climax. It could break wide open at any moment.

Sometimes God seems to be working ever so slowly, and we grow impatient for action. But when the time comes, God moves. Meanwhile, remember, God is not in a hurry. We need to exercise patience as we wait for great things—just ahead.

17

It Wasn't Raining
When Noah Built the Ark

For reasons which I have already presented, I am convinced that the Ark of Noah is resting on Mt. Ararat, sufficiently preserved to prove its real identity to unbiased people. I believe *Noah pitched it*, as God instructed him, and *God parked it* to preserve it for posterity and in God's time to present it to the world as a final warning that Jesus is coming again.

This information is unique. It produces a confrontation which demands a decision—a decision that will determine the direction in which a person will move. Literally millions are approaching the most important crossroad of their lives. Actually the path ahead is like a "Y" in the road. $\gg\!\!-\!\!\!\!-\!\!<$ There is no "straight ahead"; a choice must be made. *A crossroad demands decision; decision determines direction;* and *direction determines destiny.*

Someone has said, "The sum total of the wisdom of the ages is to find out which way God is going and walk with Him." That statement is so loaded with meaning, it merits meditation. If the Ark is uncovered, there will be multitudes of people, from students to scientists—to preachers to laymen, who will be confronted with the necessity of changing their direction.

Is the Ark up there or isn't it? If it is, then what about the Second Coming of Christ? If Christ is coming, am I ready? If I am not, then what will happen to me? A serious-minded person who isn't afraid to think about life after death will face these questions while there is still time to find answers and make decisions. Every other person will face them when it is too late for a decision. Answers are available as millions have found out.

Even if the Ark isn't there (and we do not have the absolute scientific proof that it is—yet) one still has to face the same soul-searching questions that this whole matter brings to mind. One cannot get away from the clear warning of Jesus, "As it was in the days of Noah, so shall it be at the coming of the Son of man." With or without the Ark to give added evidence, one must still answer the questions concerning the possibility of the Lord's return and judgment for unbelievers.

Suppose one makes the wrong decision and, like the people of Noah's day, finds out too late that he was wrong. Can one afford to take the chance that he might be wrong?

Would not the prudent man consider all the options and then take such action as would leave him on the right side, no matter how the debatable items turned out? In matters involving eternity, time is of the essence. Though one lives in *Time*, he is never more than a heartbeat away from *Eternity*. Therefore, procrastination, resulting in failure to make a reservation may, in the final analysis, be exactly the same as making a willful decision to reject God's offer.

In this context, the Ark is no wooden vessel and the judgment is not water. Rather, The Ark is the "Ark of Safety"— Jesus Christ (received by faith as Saviour and Lord) and the judgment is by fire. Furthermore, since we have no guarantee of tomorrow, the time for decision is NOW!

Remember: IT WASN'T RAINING WHEN NOAH BUILT THE ARK.

Appendage

Some Do, Some Don't,
Some Will and Some Won't.

I walked into the Hertz Car rental office in downtown Los Angeles—right across the street from the Hilton. After making a reservation for a car I needed to keep my various speaking engagements in the area, I reached into my pocket and pulled out a plastic tube in which I keep a tiny piece of tar-soaked wood that was brought down from Mt. Ararat. It had been given to me by Search Foundation.

As I held it toward the two ladies behind the counter, I said, "I have something more rare than moon rocks." Immediately I had their undivided attention. Then I went on, "I believe this is a piece of Noah's Ark and that the Ark will soon be uncovered for all the world to see."

They wanted to know more and I explained briefly what it was all about. Then I got down to important things. "You know we are all sinners, just like the people of Noah's day were. The apostle Paul said: 'All have sinned, and come short of the glory of God. . . . There is none righteous, no not one.' "

At that point, 50 percent of my audience retired to her desk in the back of the room. The other young lady wanted to know more.

To her I said: "The Bible says that the penalty for sin is death but God loves us and doesn't want us to perish, so He sent His Son to die in our place." I quoted John 3:16:

> For God so loved the world, that he gave his only begotten son, that whosoever believeth in him should not perish, but have everlasting life.

Then I continued: "God also said that whosoever would call upon the name of the Lord would be saved. I've seen it happen many times and I know it works. Peace comes to the heart of any person who by faith invites Jesus into his heart. The Bible calls this being 'born again' or being 'saved.' Wouldn't you like to invite Jesus into your heart and have the assurance of the forgiveness of your sins and the gift of eternal life. It's all yours in Christ."

The young lady had listened with rapt attention. In response to my question, she said, "You mean right now?"

I answered, "There's no time better than right now."

"You mean—right here?"

"There's no place better than right here."

She smiled and slowly responded, "Well, all right." To make it easier for her I offered to pray the words before her but I cautioned her not to say a word she didn't really mean. To this she quickly agreed. So I prayed and she repeated after me in this fashion:

Dear Lord,	— Dear Lord,
I am a sinner	— I am a sinner
I can't save myself	— I can't save myself.
But I want to be saved	— But I want to be saved
I believe Your Word	— I believe Your Word
and I am asking You	— and I am asking You
to save me now.	— to save me now.
Dear Jesus, come into my heart	— Dear Jesus, come into my heart
wash my sin away	— wash my sin away
and give me the gift of eternal life.	— and give me the gift of eternal life.
Thank You, Lord.	— Thank You, Lord.
In Jesus' name,	— In Jesus' name,
Amen.	— Amen.

Then I prayed alone and thanked the Lord for the privilege of being present at the birth of a soul. I prayed that she might love and serve the Lord faithfully the rest of her life, and so forth. I thanked the Lord that He does not lie and, therefore, we can rest on His promises.

When I finished, I opened my eyes to see her smiling. Next to me was another customer who had come in during my "presentation." At this point I saw he was smiling, too—with tears running down his cheeks. The young lady said to him, "Don't cry." She was still smiling. As I left I noticed the other lady behind her desk look frustrated, nervous and unhappy.

Like I said, some do and some don't. Each one must decide for himself.

Anyone interested further in information on how to be saved, may write for free literature to:
The Nathan Meyer Bible Prophecy Association
190 Loveman Avenue
Worthington, Ohio 43085

ADDITIONAL SUGGESTED BACKGROUND READING

Cummings, Violet. *Noah's Ark: Fact or Fable?* Old Tappen, N.J., Fleming H. Revell Co.

LaHaye, Tim, and Morris, John. *The Ark on Ararat.* Nashville, Tenn., Thomas Nelson Co.

Morris, John. *Adventure on Ararat.* San Diego, Calif., Creation Life Publishers.

Montgomery, John. *The Quest for Noah's Ark.* Minneapolis, Minn., Bethany Fellowship, Inc.

Navarra, Fernand. *Noah's Ark, I Touched It.* Plainfield, N.J., Logos International.

Patten, Donald. *Biblical Flood and the Ice Epoch.* Grand Rapids, Mich., Baker Book House.

Rehwinkel, A. M. *The Flood.* St. Louis, Mo., Concordia Publishing House.

Segraves, Kelly. *The Great Dinosaur Mistake.* San Diego, Calif., Beta Books.

Whitcomb, John, and Morris, Henry. *The Genesis Flood.* Philadelphia, Pa., The Presbyterian and Reformed Publishing Co.

Whitcomb, John. *The Early Earth.* Winona Lake, Ind., BMH Books.

Whitcomb, John. *The World That Perished.* Winona Lake, Ind., BMH Books.